100 Delicious Crepe and Pancake Recipes

100 EXQUISITE AND VERSATILE CRÊPE AND PANCAKE RECIPES

Lisa Simpson

Copyright Material ©2023

All Rights Reserved

No part of this book may be used or transmitted in any form or by any means without the proper written consent of the publisher and copyright owner, except for brief quotations used in a review. This book should not be considered a substitute for medical, legal, or other professional advice.

TABLE OF CONTENTS

TABLE OF CONTENTS 3
INTRODUCTION 6
CRÊPES 7
   1. Blueberry-Lemon Crêpes 8
   2. Pear Crêpes with Macadamia Cheese 10
   3. Strawberry Crêpes 13
   4. Crêpes with Plum Butter 15
   5. Banana creme Crêpes 17
   6. Cherry Crêpes 19
   7. Kumquat-pecan Crêpes 21
   8. Tropical fruit Crêpes 24
   9. Lemon Crêpes 26
   10. Crêpes With Chablis Fruit Sauce 29
   11. Ambrosia Crêpes 31
   12. Berry Crêpes with orange sauce 33
   13. Apricot-lavender Crêpes 35
   14. Saffron Crêpes 38
   15. Pansy pancakes 40
   16. Herb Crêpes 42
   17. Oreo Breakfast Crêpes 44
   18. Ice Cream Crêpes 46
   19. Suzette-Inspired Ice Cream Crêpes 48
   20. Red Velvet Crêpes with Cream Cheese Filling 50
   21. Tiramisu Crêpes 52
   22. Hazelnut Crêpes with coffee ice cream 55
   23. Hot fudge Crêpes 58
   24. Meringue filled Crêpes 60
   25. Butterscotch orange Crêpes 62
   26. Microgreen Crêpes 65
   27. Mushrooms Chickpea Crêpes 67
   28. Cheesy spinach Crêpes 69
   29. Ube Crêpes 72
   30. Eggplant-stuffed Crêpes 74
   31. Tofu Crêpes 76
   32. Lentil & Fenugreek Crêpes 78
   33. Chickpea Flour Crêpes 80
   34. Cream of Wheat Crêpes 82
   35. Bacon and egg Crêpes 84
   36. Beef stroganoff Crêpes 86
   37. BBQ pork with corn Crêpes 88

38. Ham and apple Crêpes 92
39. Egg, ham, and cheese Crêpes 94
40. Deli Turkey Crêpe 96
41. Mexican chicken Crêpes 98
42. Curried chicken Crêpes 100
43. Cheesy tuna Crêpes 102
44. Curried seafood Crêpes 104
45. Layered shrimp Crêpe 106
46. Scallops and Mushroom Crêpes 108
47. Smoked salmon Crêpe spirals 110
48. Raw Banana Flax Crêpes 112
49. Raw Apple Crêpes 114
50. Raw Chocolate Raspberry Crêpes 116

PANCAKES 119
51. Red velvet pancakes 120
52. Dark chocolate pancakes 122
53. Pineapple upside-down pancakes 125
54. Lemon meringue pancakes 128
55. Cinnamon roll pancakes 131
56. Kefir pancakes 134
57. Cottage cheese pancakes 136
58. Oatmeal pancakes 138
59. 3-Ingredient pancakes 140
60. Almond butter pancakes 142
61. Tiramisu pancakes 144
62. Lemon blueberry pancakes 147
63. Quinoa pancakes 150
64. Greek yogurt oatmeal pancakes 152
65. Gingerbread pancakes 154
66. Greek yogurt pancakes 157
67. Oatmeal raisin cookie pancakes 159
68. Peanut butter and jelly pancakes 162
69. Bacon pancakes 164
70. Raspberry almond pancakes 167
71. Peanut, banana & chocolate pancakes 170
72. Vanilla coconut pancakes 172
73. Chocolate coconut almond pancakes 175
74. Strawberry shortcake pancakes 178
75. Peanut butter cup pancakes 181
76. Mexican chocolate pancakes 183
77. Birthday surprise pancakes 185

78. Green monster pancakes 187
79. Vanilla matcha pancakes 190
80. Piña colada pancakes 192
81. Cherry almond pancakes 194
82. Key lime pancakes 196
83. Pumpkin spice pancakes 198
84. Chocolate banana pancakes 200
85. Vanilla almond pancakes 202
86. Funky monkey pancakes 204
87. Vanilla pancakes 206
88. Blueberry mango pancakes 208
89. Mocha pancakes 210
90. Chai pancakes 212
91. Carrot cake pancakes 215
92. Honey banana pancakes 218
93. Banana blueberry pancakes 220
94. Apple cinnamon pancakes 222
95. Strawberry cheesecake pancakes 224
96. Blueberry pancakes 226
97. Strawberry banana pancakes 228
98. Peaches and cream pancakes 230
99. Banana bread pancakes 232
100. Tropical pancakes 234

CONCLUSION **237**

INTRODUCTION

Crepes and pancakes are beloved breakfast dishes that can be enjoyed in many different ways. From sweet to savory, they can be filled with a variety of ingredients and topped with your favorite toppings. The delicate and thin texture of crepes make them perfect for a light breakfast or dessert, while pancakes are a classic breakfast staple with a fluffy texture that's sure to satisfy.

Fluffy, Sweet, Savory, Versatile, Delicious, Brunch, Breakfast, Easy, Quick, Family-friendly, Classic, Comforting, Creative, Homemade, Traditional, International, Fruit, Chocolate, Nutella, Cinnamon, Blueberry, Banana, Apple, Lemon, Cheese, Bacon, Sausage, Ham, Spinach, Mushroom, Feta, Ricotta, Whipped cream, Syrup, Honey, Jam, Buttermilk, Gluten-free, Dairy-free, Vegetarian, Vegan, Healthy, Indulgent, Impressive, Perfect, Tips, Tricks

Whether you're looking for a simple and classic recipe or something a little more creative, there are countless options to choose from. So, let's get cooking and explore some delicious crepe and pancake recipes!

CRÊPES

1. Blueberry-Lemon Crêpes

Makes: 6 Servings

INGREDIENTS:
- 3-ounce package of cream cheese softened
- 1½ cups half-and-half
- 1 Tablespoon lemon juice
- 3¾ package instant lemon pudding mix
- ½ cup biscuit baking mix
- 1 egg, beaten
- 6 Tablespoons milk
- 1 cup blueberry pie filling

INSTRUCTIONS:
a) Combine cream cheese, half-and-half, lemon juice, and dry pudding mix in a bowl.
b) Beat with an electric mixer on low speed for 2 minutes.
c) Refrigerate for 30 minutes. Lightly grease a 6" skillet and place over medium-high heat.
d) In a bowl, combine the biscuit baking mix, egg, and milk. Beat until smooth.
e) Pour 2 tablespoons of batter into the skillet for each Crêpe.
f) Rotating the skillet quickly, allow the batter to cover the bottom of the skillet.
g) Cook each Crêpe until lightly golden, then flip, cooking again until just golden.
h) Spoon 2 tablespoonfuls of cream cheese mixture onto each Crêpe and roll up.
i) Top with remaining cream cheese mixture and pie filling.

2. Pear Crêpes with Macadamia Cheese

Makes: 8 large crêpes

INGREDIENTS:

CRÊPES
- 2 tablespoons olive oil, plus more for oiling the frying pan
- 1½ cups all-purpose gluten-free flour
- 1½ cups almond milk
- 2 tablespoons finely ground flaxseed whisked into 6 tablespoons water
- 1 teaspoon baking soda
- Pinch unrefined sea salt

CARDAMOM PEAR TOPPING
- 4 medium pears, cored and sliced
- Pinch ground cardamom
- ½ cup filtered water, divided
- 2 tablespoons organic cane sugar
- 1 tablespoon tapioca flour

CREAM CHEESE TOPPING
- Macadamia Cream Cheese

INSTRUCTIONS:

a) For the crêpe batter, in a large bowl combine the 2 tablespoons oil, flour, almond milk, flaxseed-water mixture, baking soda, and salt, and whisk together.

b) In a large frying pan over medium heat, add enough oil to grease the entire bottom of the pan, and pour enough crêpe batter to thinly coat the pan. Cook for approximately 1 minute or until the bubbles disappear, and flip. Repeat with the remaining batter until the batter is all used up.

c) For the topping, in a medium frying pan over low to medium heat, add the pears, cardamom, and ¼ cup of water. Cook for approximately 5 minutes or until the pears are slightly softened. In a small glass bowl, combine the remaining ¼ cup of water, sugar, and tapioca until they are well mixed.

d) Add the sugar-tapioca mixture to the pears, stirring constantly. Allow cooking for another minute or until the sauce has thickened.

e) Top each crêpe with ⅛ of the pear mixture and ⅛ of the macadamia cream cheese. Serve immediately.

3. Strawberry Crêpes

Makes: 6 Servings

INGREDIENTS:
- Butter to fry Crêpes
- 3 large eggs
- ⅔ cup heavy cream
- 3 tablespoons Dr. Atkins Bake Mix
- 4 tablespoons sugar substitute
- ⅛ teaspoon almond extract
- ¼ teaspoon vanilla extract
- ½ teaspoon orange zest grated

STRAWBERRY FILLING:
- 2 cups strawberries, washed, hulled, and sliced
- 6 tablespoons Sugar Twin sugar substitute

INSTRUCTIONS:
a) Prepare a heavy, 8-inch skillet or Crêpe pan with heated butter. Whisk all Crêpe ingredients together in a mixing bowl.
b) Once the butter stops foaming, pour 1/6 Crêpe mixture into the skillet, making sure to cover the bottom evenly.
c) Cook until the bottom is browned and the top is set. Use a spatula to flip the Crêpe and brown the other side. Once done, transfer to a paper towel.
d) Repeat this procedure with the remaining batter and butter.
e) Next, make your filling by combining strawberries with sugar substitute and spoon about 1 mixture on each Crêpe.
f) Add light whipped cream to taste and garnish with remaining strawberries.

4. Crêpes with Plum Butter

Makes: 4

INGREDIENTS:
- 355ml can of club soda
- 1.5 cups of plant-milk
- 2 tablespoons canola oil
- 2 cups of AP flour
- pinch of salt
- oil for greasing the pan
- plum butter for filling

INSTRUCTIONS:
a) In a mixing bowl, whisk together all of the ingredients, except the oil and plum butter.
b) Preheat a frying pan over high heat for 2-4 minutes, or until very hot.
c) Reduce heat to medium-high after lightly brushing the frying pan with oil.
d) Pour a thin layer of batter into the pan and spread it evenly across the bottom.
e) Flip the Crêpe once the edges begin to peel away from the pan and cook for another minute or two.
f) Transfer the Crêpes to a plate and set aside to cool for a few minutes.
g) Cover them with a small amount of plum butter and roll or fold them into a triangle.

5. Banana creme Crêpes

Makes: 6 Servings

INGREDIENTS:
- 4 Bananas, divided use
- 8-ounce container of cream caramel
- Flavored yogurt
- ½ cup Whipped cream or frozen
- Non-dairy whipped topping,
- Thawed, plus additional for
- Garnish
- 6 Ready-made Crêpes
- Maple or chocolate syrup

INSTRUCTIONS:
a) Place 2 bananas in a food processor or blender, and blend until smooth.
b) Add yogurt, and blend. Stir in whipped topping.
c) Slice the remaining bananas into coins. Set aside, 12 slices for topping.
d) Place Crêpe on each serving plate: divide the yogurt mixture over each Crêpe.
e) Divide remaining banana slices and whipped cream or topping.
f) Drizzle syrup over each Crêpe.

6. Cherry Crêpes

Makes: 10 Servings

INGREDIENTS:
- 1 cup Sour cream
- ⅓ cup Brown sugar, firmly packed
- 1 cup Biscuit mix
- 1 Egg
- 1 cup Milk
- 1 can Cherry pie filling
- 1 teaspoon Orange extract

INSTRUCTIONS:
a) Blend sour cream and brown sugar, and set aside. Combine biscuit mix, egg, and milk.
b) Mix until smooth. Heat oiled 6" skillet.
c) Fry 2 Tablespoons biscuit mixture at a time until lightly brown, turn, and brown.
d) Fill each Crêpe with a portion of the sour cream mixture. Roll up.
e) Place the seam side down in the baking dish. Pour cherry pie filling overall.
f) Bake at 350~ for 5 minutes. Pour orange extract over Crêpes, and ignite to serve.

7. Kumquat-pecan Crêpes

Makes: 1 batch

INGREDIENTS:
- ½ cup Preserved kumquat
- 3 large Egg
- 1½ cups Pecans, diced
- ¾ cup Sugar
- ¾ cup Butter, room temp
- 3 tablespoons Cognac
- ½ cup Pecans, diced
- ¼ cup Sugar
- ¼ cup Butter, melted
- ½ cup Cognac

INSTRUCTIONS:
FOR FILLING:
a) Seed, chop, and pat dry kumquats, reserving ⅓ cup kumquat syrup.
b) Combine eggs, 1½ cups pecans, ¾ cup sugar, ¾ cup butter, kumquats, and 3 tablespoons Cognac in a processor or blender and mix well using on/off turns. Turn into a bowl.
c) Cover and freeze for at least 1 hour.

TO ASSEMBLE:
d) Generously butter two 7x11-inch baking dishes.
e) Reserve ⅓ cup filling for sauce. Fill each Crêpe with about 1 ½ to 2 tablespoons of filling. Roll Crêpes up cigar fashion.
f) Arrange seam side down in single layer in prepared baking dishes.
g) Preheat oven to 350 deg. Sprinkle Crêpes with remaining pecans and sugar and drizzle with melted butter.
h) Bake until bubbling hot, about 15 minutes.
i) Meanwhile, combine ⅓ cup reserved filling, 2 tablespoons Cognac, and ⅓ cup reserved kumquat syrup in a small saucepan and bring to a simmer over low heat.
j) Warm the remaining Cognac in a small saucepan.
k) To serve, arrange Crêpes on a platter and top with sauce. Ignite Cognac and pour over the top, shaking the platter until the flame subsides. Serve immediately.

8. Tropical fruit Crêpes

Makes: 4 servings

INGREDIENTS:
- 4 ounces Plain flour, sifted
- 1 pinch Salt
- 1 teaspoon Caster sugar
- 1 egg, plus one yolk
- ½ pint Milk
- 2 tablespoons Melted butter
- 4 ounces Sugar
- 2 tablespoons Brandy or rum
- 2½ cups tropical fruit mix

INSTRUCTIONS:
a) To make the Crêpe batter, place the flour, salt, and caster sugar in a bowl and mix.
b) Gradually beat in the eggs, milk, and butter. Leave to stand for at least 2 hours.
c) Heat a lightly greased frying pan, stir the batter, and use to make 8 Crêpes. Keep warm.
d) To make the filling, place the tropical fruit mix in a saucepan with the sugar and heat gently until the sugar dissolves.
e) Bring to a boil and heat until the sugar caramelizes. Add the brandy.
f) Fill each Crêpe with the fruit and serve immediately with cream or creme fraiche.

9. Lemon Crêpes

Makes: 6 Servings

INGREDIENTS:
- 1 large Egg
- ½ cup Milk
- ¼ cup All-purpose flour
- 1 teaspoon Sugar
- 1 teaspoon Grated lemon zest
- 1 pinch Salt
- Butter or oil for skillet

LEMON SAUCE:
- 2 cups Water
- 1 cup Sugar
- 2 Lemons, sliced paper thin, seeded

CREAM FILLING:
- 1 cup Heavy cream, cold
- 2 teaspoons Sugar
- 1 Teaspoon vanilla extract

INSTRUCTIONS:
CRÊPE BATTER:
a) Whisk egg and milk lightly together in a medium mixing bowl.
b) Add flour, sugar, lemon zest, and salt and whisk until smooth.
c) Refrigerate covered for at least 2 hours or overnight.

LEMON SAUCE:
d) Heat water and sugar in a heavy medium saucepan until sugar dissolves.
e) Add lemon slices and simmer for 30 minutes. Cool to room temperature.

MAKE CRÊPES:
f) Coat the Crêpe pan on a 6-inch nonstick skillet with a thin layer of butter or oil.
g) Heat pan over medium-high heat.
h) Pour in 2 tablespoons of the Crêpe batter and quickly tilt the pan to spread the batter evenly.

i) Cook until the bottom is golden and the edge has pulled away from the side of the pan, about 3 minutes.
j) Turn Crêpe and cook the second side for about 1 minute.
k) Let cool on a plate and repeat with the remaining batter to make 8 Crêpes in all.
l) Just before serving, make the cream filling: beat cream, sugar, and vanilla in a mixer bowl until stiff peaks form.
m) Place 2 Crêpes, golden side down, on each dessert plate.
n) Spoon cream filling onto each Crêpe and roll up, folding in edges and placing seam side down on plates.
o) Pour ¼ cup lemon sauce over each serving, and serve at once.

10. Crêpes With Chablis Fruit Sauce

Makes: 4 servings

INGREDIENTS:
- 3 Eggs
- 1 cup Skim milk
- 1 cup Flour
- ⅛ teaspoon Salt
- Cooking spray
- ½ cup Chablis wine
- ¼ cup Water
- ¼ cup Sugar
- 1 tablespoon Cornstarch
- ¾ cup Fresh or frozen strawberries
- ½ cup Diced orange segments
- 1 tablespoon Water
- 4 Lovers Crêpes

INSTRUCTIONS:

a) Combine the first 4 ingredients and mix on low speed for about a minute. Scrape down sides and blend well until smooth.

b) Let stand 30 minutes. Coat the bottom of 6½ inch omelet or frying pan with cooking spray.

c) Heat pan over low heat.

d) Pour in about 3 tablespoons of batter-tilting and turning pan to spread batter evenly.

e) Cook until lightly browned on the bottom-turn over and brown the other side.

f) To store-wrap Crêpes separated with waxed paper, freeze or refrigerate.

CHABLIS FRUIT SAUCE:

g) In a small saucepan, combine the first 3 ingredients-bring to a boil-simmer for 5 minutes.

h) Stir cornstarch and 1 tablespoon water until smooth.

i) Stir into wine mixture and simmer for several minutes until thickened, stirring occasionally.

j) Add fruit and heat until the fruit is hot. Fill Crêpes, fold over, and spoon extra sauce over top.

11. Ambrosia Crêpes

Makes: 1 Serving

INGREDIENTS:
- 4 Crêpes
- 16-ounce can fruit cocktail
- 1 can Frozen dessert topping - thawed
- 1 small Ripe banana sliced
- ½ cup Miniature marshmallows
- ⅓ cup Shredded coconut

INSTRUCTIONS:
a) Garnish with additional topping and fruit.
b) To freeze Crêpes stack with waxed paper between.
c) Wrap in heavy foil or freezer paper.
d) Heat in a 350° oven for 10-15 minutes.

12. Berry Crêpes with orange sauce

Makes: 4 servings

INGREDIENTS:
- 1 cup Fresh blueberries
- 1 cup Sliced strawberries
- 1 tablespoon Sugar
- Three 3-ounce packs of Cream cheese softened
- ¼ cup Honey
- ¾ cup Orange juice
- 8 Crêpes

INSTRUCTIONS:
a) Combine blueberries, strawberries, and sugar in a small bowl, and set aside.
b) To prepare sauce, beat cream cheese and honey until light, and slowly beat in orange juice.
c) Spoon about ½ cup of berry filling in the center of 1 Crêpe. Spoon about 1 tablespoon of sauce over the berries. Roll up, and place on serving plate. Repeat with remaining Crêpes.
d) Pour remaining sauce over Crêpes.

13. Apricot-lavender Crêpes

Makes: 6 Servings

INGREDIENTS:
- 1½ tablespoon Butter
- ½ cup Milk
- 1½ tablespoon Peanut oil
- 6½ tablespoons All-purpose flour
- 1 tablespoon Sugar, generous
- 1 Egg
- ⅓ teaspoon Fresh lavender blossoms
- 14 Dried apricots, Turkish
- 1 cup Riesling wine
- 1 cup Water
- 1½ teaspoon Orange zest, grated
- 3 tablespoons Honey
- ½ cup Riesling wine
- ½ cup Water
- 1 cup Sugar
- 1 tablespoon Orange zest
- ½ tablespoon Lime zest
- 1 teaspoon Fresh lavender blossoms
- 1 pinch Cream of tartar
- Flavored whipped cream, optional
- Lavender sprigs, for garnish

INSTRUCTIONS:

Crêpe BATTER

a) Melt butter over moderate heat.
b) Continue to heat until the butter is a light brown color.
c) Add milk and warm slightly.
d) Transfer the mixture to a bowl. Beat in remaining ingredients until smooth.
e) Refrigerate for an hour or more.
f) Cook Crêpes, stacking with plastic wrap or parchment in between to prevent sticking.

g) Refrigerate until ready to use.

APRICOT FILLING

h) Combine all ingredients in a saucepan.
i) Simmer for about a half hour, or until the apricots are soft.
j) Puree the mixture in a food processor until almost smooth. Cool.

RIESLING SAUCE

k) Combine all ingredients in a saucepan.
l) Bring to a boil, stirring until sugar is dissolved.
m) Brush down the sides of the saucepan with a brush dipped in cold water to prevent crystallization.
n) Cook, brushing down occasionally, to 240 degrees F. on a candy thermometer.
o) Remove from the flame and plunge the bottom of the pot into ice water to stop cooking.
p) Chill.

TO SERVE

q) Roll 3 tablespoons of filling inside each Crêpe, allowing two Crêpes per portion.
r) Line up Crêpes inside a buttered baking dish.
s) Cover with foil buttered on the inside. Heat in a 350-degree F. oven.
t) Transfer Crêpes to serving plates. Ladle sauce over and around Crêpes.
u) Garnish with whipped cream if desired, and lavender sprigs.

14. Saffron Crêpes

Makes: 12 eight-inch Crêpes

INGREDIENTS:
- 2 pinches saffron
- 2 eggs
- ¾ cup milk
- ½ cup water
- ½ teaspoon salt
- 2 to 3 tablespoons melted butter or light olive oil
- 1 cup unbleached flour
- 3 to 4 basil leaves, finely sliced

INSTRUCTIONS:
a) Cover saffron threads with a spoonful of hot water in a small bowl. Set aside.
b) Combine eggs, milk, ½ cup water, salt, butter, and flour in a blender. Process briefly and scrape down sides. Process for 10 seconds longer. Pour into a large bowl. Stir in saffron and basil.
c) Let rest, covered, for 1 hour or longer. Make Crêpes in a Crêpe pan using the manufacturer's directions.
d) To make the batter by hand, cover saffron threads with a spoonful of hot water in a small bowl. Set aside.
e) Beat eggs lightly in a large bowl. Stir in milk, ½ cup water, salt, butter, or light olive oil. Whisk in flour. Stir just enough to combine ingredients and strain.
f) Stir in saffron and basil. Let rest for 30 minutes. Make Crêpes in a Crêpe pan.
g) Stack Crêpes to keep warm or prepare in advance, wrap in foil, and store in the refrigerator. Reheat, wrapped in foil, in the oven.

15. Pansy pancakes

Makes: 12 Crêpes

INGREDIENTS
- 1½ cups milk
- ½ cup water
- 1 tablespoon sugar
- ¼ teaspoon salt
- 3 tablespoons unsalted butter, melted
- ½ cup buckwheat flour
- ¾ cup all-purpose flour
- 3 eggs
- 12 pansy flowers
- Pansy simple syrup or flower syrup of any kind, for topping, if desired

INSTRUCTIONS:
a) Place all ingredients except pansy flowers in a blender. Blend until smooth.
b) Refrigerate for at least 2 hours and up to overnight.
c) Let batter come to room temperature before frying. Shake well.
d) Heat a nonstick skillet, and melt butter.
e) Lift the skillet from heat and pour ¼ cup of the batter in the middle, tilting and swirling the pan to distribute it quickly and evenly. Return to heat.
f) After about 1 minute, sprinkle with pansies.
g) Use a spatula to loosen the edges of the Crêpe from the sides of the skillet.
h) Flip the Crêpe and cook for another 30 seconds.
i) Turn or slide it onto a serving plate. Repeat with the remaining batter.

16. Herb Crêpes

Makes: 12 Servings

INGREDIENTS:
- 1¼ cup All-purpose flour
- 1½ cup Skim milk
- 1 tablespoon Margarine, melted
- 1 Egg
- Vegetable cooking spray
- 1 tablespoon Minced fresh parsley
- 1 tablespoon Minced fresh oregano
- 1 tablespoon Minced fresh basil

INSTRUCTIONS:
a) Use Basic Crêpe Recipe below and add 1 tablespoon minced fresh parsley, 1 tablespoon minced fresh oregano, and 1 tablespoon minced fresh basil to milk mixture for these herb Crêpes.
b) Basic Crêpes: Place flour in a medium bowl.
c) Combine milk, margarine, and egg, and add the mixture to the flour, stirring with a wire whisk until almost smooth. Cover batter, and chill for 1 hour.
d) Coat an 8-inch Crêpe pan or nonstick skillet with vegetable cooking spray, and place over medium-high heat until hot.
e) Remove pan from heat, and pour a scant ¼ cup batter into pan, quickly tilt pan in all directions so batter covers pan with a thin film. Cook for about 1 minute.
f) Carefully lift the edge of Crêpe with a spatula to test for doneness.
g) Turn Crêpe over, and cook for 30 seconds on the other side.
h) Place the Crêpe on a towel, and allow it to cool. Repeat the procedure until all of the batters are used. Stack Crêpes between single layers of wax paper or paper towels to prevent sticking.

17. Oreo Breakfast Crêpes

Makes: 4 servings

INGREDIENTS:
- 1 cup flour
- 3 eggs
- 1 cup milk
- 1 ¼ cup water
- ⅛ teaspoon salt
- Oreo cookies
- Fillings for Crêpes: Nutella, Raspberry Jam, Whip Cream

INSTRUCTIONS:
a) Add the following ingredients to the mixing bowl: eggs, flour, water, milk, and salt.
b) Mix using the cage attachment until smooth, Then let the batter rest for 5 minutes or up to 24 hours in the fridge.
c) Heat and grease the pan using ½ teaspoon of oil.
d) Heat a 5-inch pan until hot.
e) Place one Oreo cookie in the middle of the pan.
f) Pour about ¼ cup of batter around the Oreo cookie.
g) Cook for 1 to 2 minutes, until the Crêpe, is golden on the bottom.
h) Use a knife, or spatula to lift the Crêpe and quickly flip it over.
i) Cook the second side for about ½ minute or until golden.
j) Fill each Crêpe with the filling of your choice.
k) Spread Nutella around the Oreo, and roll it into a cylinder.

18. Ice Cream Crêpes

Makes: 4 servings

INGREDIENTS:
- 1½ pints vegan vanilla ice cream, softened
- Vegan Dessert Crêpes
- 2 tablespoons vegan margarine
- ¼ confectioners' sugar
- ¼ cup fresh orange juice
- 1 tablespoon fresh lemon juice
- ¼ cup Grand Marnier or other orange-flavored liqueur

INSTRUCTIONS:
a) Place one-quarter of ice cream end to end on a piece of plastic wrap, wrap it up and roll it into a log with your hands.
b) Each of the ice cream logs should be rolled into a crêpe.
c) After filling the crêpes, place them in the freezer for 30 minutes to firm up.
d) Melt the margarine on a small griddle over medium heat. Pour in the sugar. Add the orange juice, lemon juice, and Grand Marnier.
e) Grill for about 2 minutes, or until most of the alcohol has evaporated.
f) To serve, arrange the filled crêpes on dessert plates and drizzle them with some orange sauce.

19. Suzette-Inspired Ice Cream Crêpes

Makes: 4 servings

INGREDIENTS:
- 1 1/2 pints vegan vanilla ice cream, softened
- Vegan Dessert Crêpes
- 2 tablespoons vegan margarine
- 1/4 confectioners' sugar
- 1/4 cup fresh orange juice
- 1 tablespoon fresh lemon juice
- 1/4 cup Grand Marnier or other orange-flavored liqueur

INSTRUCTIONS:
a) Use a large knife to cut one pint of ice cream into quarters vertically.
b) Peel away the container and discard it.
c) Arrange one whole quarter and 1/4 cup of the remaining 1/2 pint of ice cream end to end on a piece of plastic wrap, enclose it in the wrap, and use your hands to shape it into a log.
d) Repeat with the remaining ice cream to make four logs.
e) Roll each of the ice cream logs inside each of the crêpes.
f) Once the crêpes are filled, freeze them for about 30 minutes to firm up.
g) In a small skillet, heat the margarine over medium heat. Add the sugar.
h) Stir in the orange juice, lemon juice, and Grand Marnier.
i) Simmer, cooking off most of the alcohol, about 2 minutes
j) To serve, place the filled crêpes on dessert plates and spoon some of the orange sauce over each crêpe.

20. Red Velvet Crêpes with Cream Cheese Filling

Makes: 10-12 Crêpes

INGREDIENTS:
- 2 eggs
- 1 cup milk
- ½ cup water
- ½ teaspoon salt
- 3 Tablespoons butter, melted
- 1 teaspoon sugar
- 1 teaspoon vanilla extract
- 1 cup flour
- 1½ Tablespoon cocoa powder
- 5 drops of red food dye, optional
- Cream Cheese Filling/Drizzle

INSTRUCTIONS:
a) Combine eggs, milk, water, salt, sugar, vanilla, and 3 Tablespoons melted butter in a blender and pulse until foamy, about 30 seconds.
b) Add flour and cocoa powder and pulse until smooth.
c) Add the food dye at this time, if using. You will need to make the batter a little brighter than you want your final product to be.
d) Refrigerate the batter for 30 minutes or overnight.
e) When ready to prepare your Crêpes, heat 1 Tablespoon of butter in a Crêpe pan or other shallow frying pan. Ensure that the butter has coated the entire surface of the pan before adding ¼ cup of Crêpe batter and swirling to cover the surface of the pan.
f) Cook Crêpes for one minute, flip carefully, and then cook another side for half a minute.
g) Garnish with chocolate sauce and leftover cream cheese filling.

21. Tiramisu Crêpes

Makes: 10 Servings

INGREDIENTS:
- 4 large eggs
- ¾ cup 2% milk
- ¼ cup club soda
- 3 tablespoons butter, melted
- 2 tablespoons strong brewed coffee
- 1 teaspoon vanilla extract
- 1 cup all-purpose flour
- 3 tablespoons sugar
- 2 tablespoons baking cocoa
- ¼ teaspoon salt

FILLING:
- 8 ounces of mascarpone cheese
- 8 ounces of cream cheese, softened
- 1 cup sugar
- ¼ cup coffee liqueur or strong brewed coffee
- 2 teaspoons vanilla extract
- Optional: Chocolate syrup and whipped cream

INSTRUCTIONS:
a) In a large bowl, whisk eggs, milk, soda, butter, coffee, and vanilla. In another bowl, mix flour, sugar, cocoa, and salt, add to the egg mixture, and mix well. Refrigerate, covered, 1 hour.
b) Heat a lightly greased 8-in. nonstick skillet over medium heat. Stir batter. Fill a ¼-cup measure halfway with batter, and pour into the center of the pan. Quickly lift and tilt the pan to coat the bottom evenly.
c) Cook until the top appears dry, turn the Crêpe, and cook until the bottom is cooked, 15-20 seconds longer. Remove to a wire rack. Repeat with remaining batter, greasing pan as needed. When cool, stack Crêpes between pieces of waxed paper or paper towels.
d) For the filling, in a large bowl, beat cheese and sugar until fluffy. Add liqueur and vanilla, and beat until smooth. Spoon about 2 tablespoons of filling down the center of each Crêpe, and roll up. If desired, garnish with chocolate syrup and whipped cream.

22. Hazelnut Crêpes with coffee ice cream

Makes: 6 Servings

INGREDIENTS:
- ½ cup toasted hazelnuts
- ½ cup Milk
- ⅓ cup Brewed coffee, cooled
- ⅓ cup Frangelico and/or Kahlua
- 1 teaspoon Vanilla
- ⅛ teaspoon Almond extract
- 3 Eggs
- 1 cup Flour
- 3 tablespoons Unsalted butter, melted and Cooled
- Oil for pan
- 1 pint Coffee ice cream
- Caramel coffee nut sauce

INSTRUCTIONS:

a) Transfer Hazelnuts to a blender or food processor. Pulse on/off until finely chopped.

b) Combine milk, Frangelico, vanilla, almond extracts, and eggs until blended. Add flour all at once and beat until smooth and all of the flour has been absorbed. Beat in the hazelnuts, butter, and sugar. Cover and refrigerate for at least two hours, but preferably overnight.

c) Return the batter to room temperature.

d) Heat Crêpe pan until water spits across. Lightly oil and heat until hot.

e) Remove pan from heat, pour in ¼ cup batter, and swirl quickly to coat the bottom. Return pan to heat.

f) Cook until Crêpe is golden brown on the bottom, turn and cook another side.

g) Transfer to a plate, separating Crêpes with waxed paper. Repeat with remaining batter, oiling pan as needed.

h) The Crêpes can be prepared to this point ahead of time. Rewarm by removing the waxed paper, wrapping it in tin foil, and baking at a preheated 350F. oven on a cookie sheet for about 15 minutes.

i) Quickly roll warm Crêpes around small scoops of ice cream. Serve with one or both of the sauces.

23. Hot fudge Crêpes

Makes: 1 Serving

INGREDIENTS:
- 12 Chocolate Crêpes
- ⅓ cup Cocoa
- ½ cup Butter
- 1 cup Cream
- 1 cup Sugar
- 1¼ teaspoon Vanilla
- ¾ teaspoon Instant coffee
- Chocolate ice cream

INSTRUCTIONS:
a) Make Crêpe & set it aside. Melt butter in a saucepan & add sugar, coffee, & cocoa. Blend thoroughly.
b) Gradually add creme & cook over med heat, stirring constantly for about five minutes.
c) Remove from heat & add vanilla.
d) Put small scoops of ice cream on each Crêpe & fold over.
e) Pour hot fudge over Crêpes, sprinkle with chopped nuts & serve immediately.

24. Meringue filled Crêpes

Makes: 12 Servings

INGREDIENTS:
- 3 Egg whites
- ¼ teaspoon Cream of tartar
- 6 tablespoons Sugar
- ¼ teaspoon Vanilla
- 12 Basic Crêpes, cooked & ready to fill
- ¼ cup Chopped toasted almonds
- Powdered sugar
- Unsweetened cocoa powder
- Shaved chocolate
- Marmalade or berry sauce
- 2 cups Raspberries
- 3 tablespoons Sugar
- 2 tablespoons Raspberry liqueur
- ¼ cup Blackberries

INSTRUCTIONS:
a) Beat egg whites with cream of tartar to soft peaks.
b) Gradually beat in granulated sugar until stiff peaks form. Beat in vanilla. Spoon about 2 heaping tablespoons of meringue onto ½ of each Crêpe.
c) Sprinkle ½ teaspoon of almonds onto the meringue.
d) Fold Crêpe in half.
e) Place filled Crêpes on a baking sheet.
f) Bake at 400 degrees for 3 to 5 mins, just until the meringue is puffed and browned around the edges.
g) After the Crêpes have baked, sprinkle ½ teaspoon of almonds over the top of each, then sprinkle with powdered sugar and cocoa powder.
h) Garnish with a few pieces of shaved chocolate.
i) Serve with berry sauce or marmalade.

FOR SAUCE:
j) Puree 1¾ cups raspberries with sugar. Stir in liqueur. Stir in blackberries and the remaining raspberries.

25. Butterscotch orange Crêpes

Makes: 15 Servings

INGREDIENTS:
BUTTERSCOTCH ORANGE FILLING:
- 6 ounces butterscotch flavored morsels
- 8-ounce pack of cream cheese softened
- 2 teaspoons Milk
- 1 tablespoon Orange flavored liqueur

ORANGE SAUCE:
- ⅓ cup Butter
- ¼ cup Sugar
- ¼ cup Orange juice
- 1 tablespoon Orange flavored liqueur

CRÊPES:
- ¾ cup All-purpose flour
- ¾ teaspoon Salt
- 3 Eggs
- 1 cup Milk
- 2 tablespoons Butter, melted
- 1 tablespoon Grated orange rind
- Melted butter

INSTRUCTIONS:
BUTTERSCOTCH ORANGE FILLING:
a) Melt over hot water, Nestle Toll House butterscotch flavored morsels, and stir until smooth.
b) In a small bowl, beat cream cheese until smooth.
c) Gradually add melted morsels and milk, and beat until well blended.
d) Stir in orange-flavored liqueur.

ORANGE SAUCE:
e) In a small saucepan, combine butter, sugar, and orange juice.
f) Stir over medium heat until butter is melted and sugar is dissolved.
g) Stir in orange-flavored liqueur.

CRÊPES:
h) In a large bowl, combine flour and salt. Set aside. In a medium bowl, combine eggs, milk, 2 tablespoons melted butter, and grated orange rind, and beat until well blended.
i) Gradually add to flour mixture, and beat until smooth.
j) Heat an 8-inch Crêpe pan or skillet over medium heat, and brush with melted butter.
k) For each Crêpe, pour about 2 tablespoons batter into the pan, and immediately turn and tip the pan to coat the bottom. Cook for 10-15 seconds.
l) Flip Crêpe, and cook additional 5 seconds.
m) Spread 1 slightly rounded tablespoonful of Butterscotch Orange Filling over each Crêpe.
n) Fold into triangles or roll up jelly-roll fashion, and place on a serving platter.
o) Spoon Orange Sauce over Crêpes.

26. Microgreen Crêpes

Makes: 6 Crêpes

INGREDIENTS:
- 2 eggs
- ¼ cup old-fashioned oats
- ¼ cup Whole Wheat Flour
- 1 tablespoon ground flax
- ½ cup sunflower microgreens
- ½ cup milk
- ¼ cup water

INSTRUCTIONS:
a) Combine all ingredients in a blender and blend until thoroughly combined.
b) Refrigerated for at least 15 minutes.
c) Heat a non-stick pan on high heat.
d) Spray with a light coating of oil spray.
e) Pour a scant ¼ cup of batter into the pan and quickly swirl it around so it reaches the edges of the pan.
f) Cook for about 1 minute, or until the Crêpe begins to bubble and the edges begin to brown.
g) Shake the pan to loosen the Crêpe and then using a thin spatula, carefully turn the Crêpe in the pan.
h) Cook for just 10 seconds on the second side- just enough to set and very lightly brown.
i) Stack the Crêpes on a plate, one on top of the other.

27. Mushrooms Chickpea Crêpes

Makes: 6 Crêpes

INGREDIENTS:
CRÊPES:
- 140 g chickpea flour
- 30 g peanut flour
- 5 g nutritional yeast
- 5 g curry powder
- 350 ml water
- Salt, to taste

FILLING:
- 10 ml olive oil
- 4 Portobello mushroom caps, thinly sliced
- 1 onion, thinly sliced
- 30 g baby spinach
- Salt, and pepper, to taste
- Vegan mayo

INSTRUCTIONS:
MAKE THE CRÊPES
a) Combine chickpea flour, peanut flour, nutritional yeast, curry powder, water, and salt to taste in a food blender.
b) Heat a large non-stick skillet over medium-high heat. Spray the skillet with some cooking oil.
c) Pour ¼ cup of the batter into the skillet and with a swirl motion distribute the batter all over the skillet's bottom.
d) Cook the Crêpe for 1 minute per side. Slide the Crêpe onto a plate and keep warm.

MAKE THE FILLING
e) Heat olive oil in a skillet over medium-high heat.
f) Add mushrooms and onion and cook for 6-8 minutes.
g) Add spinach and toss until wilted, for 1 minute.
h) Season with salt and pepper and transfer into a large bowl.
i) Fold in prepared vegan mayo.

28. Cheesy spinach Crêpes

Makes: 4 servings

INGREDIENTS:
- 3 Eggs
- 1 cup Milk
- 1 tablespoon Melted butter
- ¾ cup All-purpose flour
- ¼ teaspoon Salt
- 2 cups Shredded Havarti, Swiss OR
- Mozzarella cheese, divided
- 2 cups Cottage OR Ricotta cheese
- ¼ cup Grated Parmesan cheese
- 1 Egg, slightly beaten
- 10-ounce pack of Frozen chopped spinach
- 300g, thawed and squeezed dry
- ¼ teaspoon Salt
- ⅛ teaspoon Pepper
- 1½ cup Tomato sauce

INSTRUCTIONS:
FOR CRÊPES:
a) Blend ingredients in a blender or food processor for 5 seconds.

b) Scrape down the sides and blend the batter for 20 seconds longer. Cover and let stand for at least 30 minutes.

c) Heat an 8-inch nonstick skillet over medium heat. Brush with melted butter. Stir batter. Pour about 3 tablespoons of batter into the pan and quickly tip the pan to coat the bottom. Cook until the bottom is slightly browned, about 45 seconds. Turn Crêpe with a spatula and cook about 20 seconds longer.

d) Transfer to a plate. Repeat with the remaining batter, brushing the pan with a little melted butter before cooking each Crêpe. *Makes:* 10 to 12 Crêpes. Select 8 Crêpes.

FOR FILLING:
e) Reserve ½ cup Havarti cheese. Combine the remaining ingredients. Place ½ cup cheese filling on each Crêpe and roll up.

f) Place seam-side down in a greased 13x9-inch baking dish. Pour tomato sauce on top. Sprinkle with reserved Havarti cheese. Bake in a 375F oven, for 20 to 25 minutes or until heated through.

29. Ube Crêpes

Makes: 30 servings

INGREDIENTS:
- 2 cups all-purpose flour
- 1 cup Rice flour
- ½ cup Ube
- 2 teaspoons Coarse salt
- 3 Egg whites
- 2 cups Water
- 2 cups Canned unsweetened coconut milk
- 1 medium Red or green leaf lettuce head
- Vegetable Filling
- Peanut Sauce

INSTRUCTIONS:
a) Whisk the dry ingredients together in a bowl, and make a well in the center. Add the egg whites, water, and coconut milk, a little at a time, incorporating them into the dry ingredients with a whisk. The batter should have the consistency of heavy cream. If it is too thick, loosen it with water.
b) Chill in the refrigerator for at least 1 hour.
c) Heat an 8-inch nonstick skillet over medium-low heat. Meanwhile, remove the batter from the refrigerator, whisk it to remove any lumps, or add water to thin it if necessary. Add about 1½ ounces of batter to the skillet. Rotate the pan so that the batter covers the entire surface. When lumpia appears dry, turn it with the aid of a rubber spatula, being careful not to let it brown. Remove from pan and set aside.
d) Place ube Crêpe on a plate with the flat side facing up. Arrange 2 overlapping lettuce leaves so that they extend over the edge on one side. Place ¼ cup of warm Vegetable Filling on the lettuce, and roll.
e) Place lumpia seam-side-down on a plate. Drizzle with Peanut Sauce. Serve immediately.

30. Eggplant-stuffed Crêpes

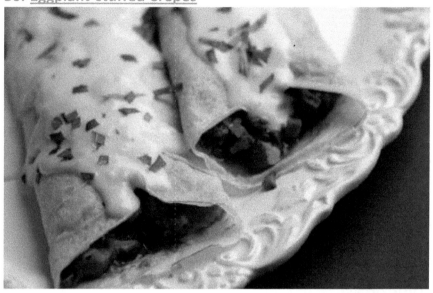

Makes: 8 servings

INGREDIENTS:
- 4 tablespoons Onion, chopped
- 4 cups Eggplant, diced, cooked
- 4 cups Tomatoes, fresh, chopped
- 1 cup Vegetable broth
- 4 tablespoons Curry powder
- 1 teaspoon Cinnamon
- 2 teaspoons Salt
- 8 Garlic cloves, chopped
- 24 Crêpes

INSTRUCTIONS:
a) Sauté all the ingredients, except the Crêpes, in a large skillet over medium heat for 10 minutes.
b) Divide the mixture evenly between the Crêpes.
c) Roll up and serve hot.
d) Top with Greek Tomato Sauce.

31. Tofu Crêpes

Makes: 10 crêpes

INGREDIENTS:
- 1 ⅓ cups plain or vanilla soy milk
- 1 cup all-purpose flour
- ⅓ cup firm tofu, drained and crumbled
- 2 tablespoons vegan margarine, melted
- 2 tablespoons sugar
- 1½ teaspoons pure vanilla extract
- ½ teaspoon baking powder
- ⅛ teaspoon salt
- Canola or other neutral oil, for cooking

INSTRUCTIONS:
a) Combine all of the ingredients
b) except the frying oil in a mixer until smooth.
c) Preheat a nonstick griddle or crêpe pan over medium-high heat.
d) Pour 3 tablespoons of batter into the griddle's center and tilt the pan to thinly spread the batter.
e) Cook until golden brown on both sides, flipping once.
f) Place the leftover batter on a tray and continue the process, oiling the pan as needed

32. Lentil & Fenugreek Crêpes

Makes: 3½ cups

INGREDIENTS:
- ½ onion, peeled and halved
- 1 cup brown basmati rice, soaked
- 2 tablespoons split gram, soaked
- ½ teaspoon fenugreek seeds, soaked
- ¼ cup whole black lentils with skin-soaked
- 1 teaspoon coarse sea salt, divided
- Oil, for pan frying
- 1½ cups water

INSTRUCTIONS:
a) Pulse the lentils and rice with water.
b) Leave the batter to ferment for 6 to 7 hours in a slightly warm place.
c) Preheat a griddle over medium heat.
d) Spread 1 teaspoon of oil in the pan.
e) Once the pan is hot, insert a fork into the onion's uncut, rounded part.
f) Rub the cut half of the onion back and forth across your pan while holding the fork handle.
g) Keep a small bowl of oil on the side with a spoon for later use.
h) Ladle batter into the center of the hot, preheated pan.
i) Make slow clockwise motions with the back of your ladle from the center to the outer edge of the pan until the batter becomes thin and crêpe-like.
j) Pour a thin stream of oil into a circle around the batter with a spoon.
k) Cook the dosa until it is slightly browned.
l) Flip and cook the other side as well.
m) Serve with spiced jeera or lemon potatoes, coconut chutney, and sambhar.

33. Chickpea Flour Crêpes

Makes: 8

INGREDIENTS:
- ½ teaspoon ground coriander
- ½ teaspoon turmeric powder
- 2 green Thai, serrano, or cayenne chiles, chopped
- ¼ cup dried fenugreek leaves
- 2 cups gram flour
- 1 teaspoon red chile powder or cayenne
- Oil, for pan frying
- 1-piece ginger root, peeled and grated or minced
- ½ cup fresh cilantro, minced
- 1 teaspoon coarse sea salt
- 1½ cups water
- 1 onion, peeled and minced

INSTRUCTIONS:
a) In a large mixing bowl, combine the flour and water until smooth. Set aside.
b) Mix in the remaining ingredients, except the oil.
c) Preheat a griddle over medium heat.
d) Spread ½ teaspoon oil over the griddle.
e) Pour batter into the center of the pan.
f) Spread the batter in a circular, clockwise motion from the center to the outside of the pan with the back of the ladle to make a thin, round pancake.
g) Cook the poora for about 2 minutes on one side, then flip it to cook on the other side.
h) With the spatula, press down to ensure that the center is also cooked through.
i) Serve with Mint or Peach Chutney on the side.

34. Cream of Wheat Crêpes

Makes: 6

INGREDIENTS:
- 3 cups cream of wheat
- 2 cups unsweetened plain soy yogurt
- 3 cups water
- 1 teaspoon coarse sea salt
- ½ teaspoon ground black pepper
- ½ teaspoon red chile powder or cayenne
- ½ yellow or red onion, peeled and finely diced
- 1 green Thai, serrano, or cayenne chile, chopped
- Oil, for pan frying, set aside in a dish
- ½ onion, peeled and halved

INSTRUCTIONS:
a) Combine the cream of wheat, yogurt, water, salt, black pepper, and red chile powder in a large mixing bowl and set aside for 30 minutes to ferment slightly.
b) Add the onion and chiles and gently combine.
c) Preheat a griddle over medium heat.
d) In the pan, heat 1 teaspoon of oil.
e) Once the pan is hot, insert a fork into the onion's uncut, rounded part.
f) Rub the cut half of the onion back and forth across your pan.
g) Keep the onion with the fork inserted handy for use between dosas.
h) Pour enough batter into the center of your hot, prepared pan.
i) Make slow clockwise motions with the back of your ladle from the center to the outer edge of the pan until the batter becomes thin and crêpe-like.
j) Pour a thin stream of oil into a circle around the batter with a spoon.
k) Cook the dosa until it is lightly browned and begins to pull away from the pan.
l) Cook the other side as well.

35. Bacon and egg Crêpes

Makes: 1 Serving

INGREDIENTS:
- 1 pound Bacon, cooked & crumbled
- 8 Eggs
- ¼ cup Heavy cream
- ¼ cup Chopped green onions
- Salt & pepper
- 1 cup Grated Monterey Jack
- 8 8\" Crêpes

INSTRUCTIONS:
a) Cut bacon into pieces & fry until crisp, drain well. Whisk eggs & cream.
b) Stir in bacon, onions & seasonings.
c) Pour into a hot buttered pan.
d) As portions cook, gently lift with a spatula so uncooked portions can flow to the bottom.
e) Sprinkle cheese over eggs when almost done.
f) Spoon egg mixture into Crêpes & roll. Serve with hash browns & green grapes.

36. Beef stroganoff Crêpes

Makes: 1 Serving

INGREDIENTS:
- 18 Crêpes
- 2 teaspoons Worcestershire sauce
- ⅓ cup Butter
- ⅓ cup Tomato sauce
- 1 Onion
- ⅓ cup Red wine
- 2 Cloves garlic
- ½ teaspoon Black pepper
- ½ pounds Mushrooms
- ⅓ cup Beef stock
- 2 pounds Rump steak
- 2 teaspoons Salt
- ¼ teaspoon Ground cumin
- 2 cups Sour cream
- ¼ teaspoon Marjoram
- Chopped chives

INSTRUCTIONS:
a) Sauté onion & garlic in butter until the onion is soft. Slice the mushrooms thinly & and pan. Cook for five minutes.
b) Cut steak into thin strips & add to the pan along with cumin, marjoram, Worcestershire & tomato sauce.
c) Stir frequently & cook until the meat browns.
d) Add the wine, stock, salt, and pepper & cook until the meat is tender.
e) Add sour cream & heat just until warm. Now fill each Crêpe with stroganoff mixture.
f) Fold over & put into a shallow buttered baking dish. Bake at 350F in the oven for 20 minutes.
g) Sprinkle with chives & serve.

37. BBQ pork with corn Crêpes

Makes: 8 servings

INGREDIENTS:
- ¼ cup Corn flour
- ¼ cup All-purpose flour
- 2 teaspoons Sugar
- ¼ teaspoon Kosher salt
- 1 Egg
- ¾ cup Milk
- 2 tablespoons Unsalted butter, melted
- 2 tablespoons Minced chives
- 2 cups Barbecue sauce
- 4 cups Shredded cooked pork
- ½ cup Minced white onion
- 2 tablespoons Lime juice, more to taste
- 1 medium Tomato
- 2 Medium, ripe avocados
- 1 Serrano chilies, finely minced
- 2 tablespoons Chopped cilantro
- Kosher salt to taste
- ¾ cup Chili sauce
- ⅓ cup Molasses
- 3 tablespoons Soy sauce
- 1 tablespoon Dijon mustard
- 1 Clove garlic, crushed
- 3 tablespoons Lemon juice
- ⅓ cup Chicken stock
- ¼ cup Water
- 1 teaspoon Tabasco sauce
- 1 teaspoon Kosher salt
- 2 teaspoons Worcestershire sauce
- ¼ teaspoon Chili flakes
- ½ Anaheim chili, seeded and cut into 1-inch pieces
- ½ Chipotle chili in adobo sauce

INSTRUCTIONS:
a) In a medium mixing bowl sift together the dry ingredients. In a separate bowl combine the egg, milk, and melted butter.
b) Make a well in the dry ingredients and gradually beat in the egg mixture.
c) Stir in the chives.
d) Let the batter rest for 30 minutes before using.
e) Heat a well-seasoned Crêpe pan over medium heat until almost smoking.
f) Butter lightly and pour in about 2 tablespoons of batter, just enough to make a thin 5-inch Crêpe, tilting the pan to distribute the batter evenly.
g) Bake until golden brown, cooking on one side only.
h) Remove the Crêpe from the pan and continue with the remaining batter, stacking the warm Crêpes on a plate.
i) Heat the barbecue sauce in a medium saucepan and add the shredded pork.
j) Stir to coat the pork evenly with the sauce. Simmer gently for a few minutes to make sure the meat is heated through. Fold or roll the Crêpes around the filling.
k) Top with any remaining barbecue sauce and serve the avocado salsa on the side.

AVOCADO SALSA
l) In a medium-sized bowl, mix the minced white onion and 2 tablespoons of lime juice.
m) Set aside while preparing the tomato and avocados.
n) Core and cut the tomato into ¼-inch dice. Cut the avocados in half, remove the seeds, and scoop out the flesh.
o) Cut the flesh into ½-inch dice. add the tomato, avocado, minced chilies, and cilantro to the onion mixture.
p) Taste for seasoning and add salt, lime juice, or minced chili as needed. Cover tightly with plastic wrap and let the salsa stand for about ½ hour before serving.

BARBECUE SAUCE

q) Combine all the ingredients in a heavy-bottomed saucepan and bring to a boil over high heat.
r) Reduce heat to low and simmer for 15 to 20 minutes.
s) Remove from heat and put through a fine strainer.
t) Refrigerate if not used immediately. The sauce will keep in the refrigerator for up to 4 days.

38. Ham and apple Crêpes

Makes: 6 Servings

INGREDIENTS:
- 3 Eggs, well beaten
- ¾ cup Milk
- ⅔ cup All-purpose flour
- ¼ cup Chopped onion
- 2 tablespoons Sweet green peppers, Seeded and minced
- ¼ cup Celery, chopped
- 2 mediums Green apples -- peeled, Cored, chop
- ½ cup All-purpose flour
- 1 cup Chicken broth
- 1 cup Light cream
- 1 teaspoon Curry powder
- 2 cups Cooked ham -- diced
- 6 tablespoons Butter

INSTRUCTIONS:
a) Beat eggs, milk, and flour until smooth, with a consistency similar to heavy cream.
b) Brush the bottom of a 6-inch skillet with butter. Spoon in 2 tablespoons batter, rotating pan to coat the bottom evenly.
c) Cook until the outer edge of the Crêpe is brown, remove from the pan, turn, and brown another side.
d) Make Crêpes until all batter is used. Melt butter. Sauté onion, celery, green pepper, and apples, stirring until tender. Sprinkle with flour, stir, and cook for one minute.
e) Gradually stir in chicken broth, cream, and curry powder.
f) Cook, stirring, until sauce boils, fold in ham. Cool slightly, and spoon ¼ cup filling on each Crêpe. Roll up and place in a heavily buttered shallow casserole.
g) Bake at 400 degrees for 15-20 minutes.

39. Egg, ham, and cheese Crêpes

Makes: 8 servings

INGREDIENTS:
- Melted clarified butter
- 2 cups Savory Buckwheat Crêpes Batter
- 8 Eggs
- 4 ounces Shredded Danish ham
- 4 ounces Shredded Monterey jack
- Cheese

INSTRUCTIONS:
a) Heat a 9- or 10-inch Crêpe pan or skillet over moderately high heat.
b) Brush generously with melted butter.
c) When butter sizzles, add ¼ cup of Buckwheat Crêpes batter and swirl to coat pan.
d) Into the center of the batter gently break one egg, keeping the yolk whole.
e) Cook just until the white is set, the yolk should remain runny.
f) Top with ½ ounce ham and ½ ounce cheese.
g) Gently fold sides of Crêpe in over cheese. Remove Crêpe to a warm plate with a spatula.
h) Continue with remaining Crêpe batter and eggs.

40. Deli Turkey Crêpe

Makes: 2

INGREDIENTS:
- 3 organic eggs
- ½ cup softened cream cheese
- ½ tablespoons stevia
- ½ teaspoon cinnamon powder
- 4 slices ham
- 4 slices deli turkey
- 1 cup Swiss cheese, grated
- 2 tablespoons organic butter, divided

INSTRUCTIONS:
a) Place the first four ingredients in a food processor and pulse until you achieve a nice batter. Set aside and let it rest for 5 minutes.
b) Melt the butter in a non-stick pan over the medium-high fire and scoop a heaping tablespoon of the batter into the pan. Move the pan side to side to create a Crêpe. Cook each side for 2 minutes.
c) Assemble the Crêpe by topping one side with 1 slice of ham, and 1 slice of deli turkey, and sprinkle with the Swiss cheese.
d) Place another Crêpe on top and do the same procedure.
e) Using the same pan, melt the remaining butter and then place the stacked Crêpe in it.
f) Cover and allow to cook for 2 minutes before flipping the Crêpe.
g) Serve warm.

41. Mexican chicken Crêpes

Makes: 4 servings

INGREDIENTS:
- 2 cups Diced cooked chicken
- 4 ounces sliced mushrooms, drained
- 2 tablespoons Diced green chiles
- ¼ cup Onion, chopped
- ¼ cup Celery, diced
- ¼ cup Toasted sliced almonds
- ½ pint Sour cream
- 10 ¾ ounce can Cream of chicken soup
- 8 Corn tortillas
- 2 tablespoons Dry sherry
- ½ cup Shredded cheddar cheese

INSTRUCTIONS:
a) Combine chicken, mushrooms, green chiles, onion, celery, almonds, sour cream, and ½ can of soup in a large bowl.
b) Mix well.
c) Place 2 tortillas on a paper towel. Cover with another towel.
d) Microwave at high until hot and pliable, 30 to 45 seconds.
e) Place ½ cup chicken mixture on tortilla Roll up jelly-roll fashion.
f) Place seam side down in a 2-quart oblong dish.
g) Repeat until all tortillas are filled. filled.
h) Combine sherry with ½ a can of soup. Spoon soup mixture over tortillas.
i) Cover with wax paper. Microwave at medium-high for 8 minutes.
j) Sprinkle cheese on top.
k) Microwave at medium-high until cheese is melted, 2 to 3 minutes.

42. Curried chicken Crêpes

Makes: 16 Servings

INGREDIENTS:
- 1 Batch Crêpes
- 4 tablespoons Butter or margarine
- 1 medium Onion, chopped
- 1 cup Celery, finely chopped
- 2 tablespoons All-purpose flour
- ½ teaspoon Salt
- ¼ teaspoon Pepper
- 2 teaspoons Curry powder
- 1 cup Chicken broth
- 3 cups Cooked chicken, diced
- ½ cup Sour cream, or heavy cream
- Chutney, chopped peanuts, bacon bits, and shredded coconut for toppings

INSTRUCTIONS:
a) Preheat oven to 375 degrees.
b) Melt butter in a large skillet, add onion and celery, and sauté until just tender-crisp.
c) Stir in flour and seasonings and cook for 5 minutes.
d) Add broth and bring to a simmer until thickened. Remove from heat and stir in chicken and sour cream.
e) Place a couple of heaping tablespoons or more across the center of each Crêpe, brown side out.
f) Roll and place seam side down in a buttered 13"x9" baking pan. Brush or drizzle with melted butter.
g) Bake for 20-25 minutes or until hot and bubbling.
h) Top with chutney, peanuts, bacon bits, and shredded coconut.

43. Cheesy tuna Crêpes

Makes: 4 servings

INGREDIENTS:
- 4 Crêpes
- ½ cup Chopped celery
- ¼ cup Chopped onion
- 7¾-ounce can tuna, drained
- 2 cups Frozen broccoli, cut up
- 2 cups Shredded Cheddar cheese

INSTRUCTIONS:
a) Place broccoli in 1½ qt. microwave-safe casserole.
b) Cover and microwave as directed, drain
c) Stir in 1 ½ cups of cheese and the remaining ingredients. Microwave covered on high for 1 minute.
d) Spoon onto Crêpes, and roll up.
e) Arrange in a square microwave dish, 8 x 8 x 2", and sprinkle with remaining cheese.
f) Cover loosely with plastic wrap and microwave on high until cheese is melted, 2 to 3 minutes⅖ Servings.

44. Curried seafood Crêpes

Makes: 1 Serving

INGREDIENTS:
- 2 cups Chicken stock
- 2 cups Dry white wine
- Salt
- ½ pounds of Sea scallops
- ½ pounds Scrod fillet
- 3 tablespoons Unsalted butter
- 2 Carrots
- 2 tablespoons All-purpose flour
- 2 teaspoons Curry powder
- 1 cup Milk
- 2 tablespoons chutney

INSTRUCTIONS:
a) In a large sauté pan bring 4 cups water to a simmer, add the scallops and the scrod, and poach the seafood. stir in the carrots, 2 tablespoons water, salt, and sugar, and cook covered, over moderate heat for 2 minutes.
b) Whisk in the flour, and cook the roux over moderately low heat, whisking for 3 minutes.
c) Whisk in the curry powder, add the milk in a stream, whisking, and salt and pepper to taste.
d) Stir in the seafood and carrot mixture, the peas, minced parsley, and enough of the poaching liquid to the desired consistency.
e) Put 2 tablespoons of mixture into each prepared Crêpe.

45. Layered shrimp Crêpe

Makes: 4 servings

INGREDIENTS:
- 8 ounces Creamy herb-garlic cheese
- 8 Crêpes
- ½ pounds Tiny cooked shrimp
- 3 tablespoons Chopped fresh chives
- 2½ cups Shredded jack cheese

INSTRUCTIONS:
a) Bring cheese to room temperature. Preheat oven to 350 degrees.
b) On each of four Crêpes: Spread two TBL garlic herb cheese.
c) Place cheese-side-up on a buttered baking sheet or oven-proof serving plate.
d) Mix shrimp, 2¼ cups of jack cheese, and chives. Divide and spread on the four Crêpes.
e) Top each with another Crêpe, and sprinkle with remaining jack cheese.
f) Bake until heated through, 30 to 35 minutes.
g) Cut into wedges and serve immediately.

46. Scallops and Mushroom Crêpes

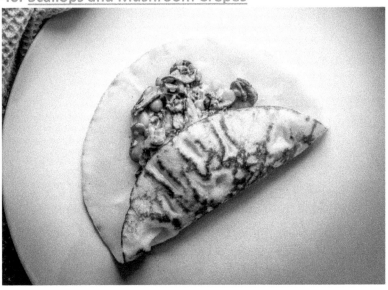

Makes: 3 servings

INGREDIENTS:
- 1 Crêpes recipe
- ½ pounds Fresh or frozen scallops
- ¾ cup whipping cream
- 1 tablespoon Flour
- dash Salt and pepper
- 2½ ounce sliced mushroom
- 2 tablespoons Dry white wine
- 1 tablespoon Snipped chives
- 2 Slices bacon, crisp-drained, crumbled.
- Snipped chives

INSTRUCTIONS:
a) Preheat Crêpes, and set aside. Thaw scallops if frozen.
b) In a saucepan cover scallops with cold water. Bring to boiling, reduce heat, and simmer for 1 minute. Drain and halve scallops. In a small saucepan gradually add whipping cream to flour, stirring till smooth.
c) Stir in salt and pepper Cook and stir over low heat till thickened and bubbly.
d) Stir in mushroom wine, 1 tbs. chives and crumbled bacon. Reserve half of the mixture.
e) Stir scallops into the remaining half of the mixture.
f) Spoon about ¼ of the scallop mixture down the center of the unbrowned side of the Crêpe, and roll up the Place seam side down, in a shallow baking dish.
g) Repeat with remaining Crêpes. Spoon the reserved wine mixture over Crêpes. Bake in a 370 F oven for 15 to 18 minutes. Sprinkle with additional chives.

47. Smoked salmon Crêpe spirals

Makes: 1 Serving

INGREDIENTS:
- ½ pounds Thinly sliced smoked salmon
- 2 tablespoons Cream cheese at room temperature
- 2 tablespoons Unsalted butter, cut into pieces, at room temperature
- 2 teaspoons Fresh lemon juice
- 2 teaspoons Snipped fresh dill
- 4 Crêpes

INSTRUCTIONS:
a) In a food processor puree half, the smoked salmon, add the cream cheese, butter, and lemon juice, and blend until the mixture is smooth.
b) Transfer the puree to a bowl and stir in the dill.
c) On the paler side of each Crêpe spread a thin ¼ of the puree mixture, top with ¼ salmon slices.
d) Roll the Crêpe tightly to enclose the filling in the Crêpe.
e) Chill seam side down, covered for at least 1 hour, or until they are firm enough to slice.
f) Slice diagonally into ¼-inch thick spirals.

48. Raw Banana Flax Crêpes

Makes: 4 Crêpes

INGREDIENTS:
- 2 whole bananas, mashed
- ½ cup flax meal
- ½ cup water, or as needed

INSTRUCTIONS:
a) Place the banana in the bottom of a high-speed blender.
b) Add the flax meal and water, and blend until smooth.
c) Spread the mixture evenly onto one lined 14-inch-square Excalibur Dehydrator tray.
d) Dehydrate for 4 to 6 hours at 104°F, or until completely dry.

49. Raw Apple Crêpes

Makes: 4 Wrappers

INGREDIENTS:
- 1 cup cored and diced apple
- ½ cup flax meal
- 2 tablespoons agave syrup
- ½ cup water, or as needed

INSTRUCTIONS:
a) Place the apples in the bottom of a high-speed blender.
b) Add the flax meal, agave, and water.
c) Blend until smooth.
d) Spread the mixture evenly onto one lined 14-inch-square Excalibur Dehydrator tray.
e) Dehydrate for 4 to 6 hours at 104°F, or until completely dry.
f) You can also flip the Crêpes, peel off the liner, and dehydrate them for another couple of hours until dry.

50. Raw Chocolate Raspberry Crêpes

Makes: 10 crêpes

INGREDIENTS:
CRÊPES SHELLS:
- ¼ cup golden flaxseeds, ground
- 1 cup hulled and sliced strawberries
- ½ cup Thai coconut meat
- ½ cup water
- 1 banana
- 1 tablespoon maple syrup
- 1 teaspoon ground cinnamon
- ½ teaspoon salt

CHOCOLATE GANACHE FILLING:
- 1½ small ripe avocados pitted and peeled
- ¼ cup pure maple syrup
- 2 tablespoons melted coconut oil
- ½ teaspoon vanilla extract
- ½ cup raw cacao powder
- 1 cup Chocolate Sauce

TO SERVE:
- 2 cups raspberries
- 1 small bunch of mint, for garnish

INSTRUCTIONS:
CRÊPE SHELLS:
a) Blend the crêpe shell ingredients until smooth, about 1 minute.
b) On a nonstick sheet, spread the crêpe batter into a thin layer and put it into the dehydrator.
c) Dehydrate the crêpe shells for 5 hours at 90°F.
d) After 5 hours, flip the nonstick sheet over and peel it away from the sheet of crêpe batter.
e) Return the sheet of crêpe batter to the dehydrator to finish drying for another 3 to 5 hours at 90°F
f) Remove and cut out 3- to 5-inch rounds with a small knife.

CHOCOLATE GANACHE FILLING:

g) In a food processor, puree the avocado flesh until smooth.
h) Add the maple syrup, melted coconut oil, and vanilla.
i) Finally, add the cacao powder and process until the chocolate is fully incorporated.
j) Refrigerate.

TO ASSEMBLE:
k) Spread a few tablespoons of the chocolate ganache down the center of each of the 10 crêpe shells.
l) Place 4 raspberries on top of each ganache stripe.
m) Roll the shell into a cylinder, using a little bit of the sticky ganache to help seal the roll overlap.
n) \Garnish with fresh mint.

PANCAKES

51. Red velvet pancakes

Ingredients:
Topping
- ½ cup plain kefir
- 2 tablespoons powdered sugar

Pancakes
- 1¾ cups old-fashioned rolled oats
- 3 tablespoons cocoa powder
- 1½ teaspoons baking powder
- 1 teaspoon baking soda
- ¼ teaspoon salt
- 3 tablespoons maple syrup
- 2 tablespoons coconut oil (melted)
- 1½ cups 2% low-fat milk
- 1 large egg
- 1 teaspoon red food coloring
- Chocolate shavings or chips, for serving

Directions

a) For the topping, add both Ingredients to a small bowl and stir until combined. Set aside.
b) For the pancakes, add all items to a high-speed blender and blitz on high to liquefy. Make sure everything is well blended.
c) Let the batter rest for 5 to 10 minutes. This allows all of the Ingredients to come together and gives the batter a better consistency.
d) Spray a non-stick skillet or griddle generously with vegetable oil and heat over medium heat.
e) Once the skillet is hot, add the batter using a ¼-cup measuring cup and pour the batter into the skillet to make the pancake. Use the measuring cup to help shape the pancake.
f) Cook until the sides appear set and bubbles form in the middle (about 2 to 3 minutes), then flip the pancake.
g) Once the pancake is cooked on that side, remove pancake from the heat and place on a plate.
h) Continue these steps with the rest of the batter.
i) Stack and serve with topping and chocolate chips.

52. Dark chocolate pancakes

Ingredients:
Filling
- 1 cup dark chocolate chips
- ½ cup heavy whipping cream

Pancakes
- 1¾ cups old-fashioned rolled oats
- 1½ teaspoons baking powder
- 1 teaspoon baking soda
- ½ teaspoon cinnamon
- ¼ teaspoon salt
- 2 tablespoons coconut oil (melted)
- 1 tablespoon maple syrup
- 1 teaspoon vanilla extract
- 1½ cups 2% low-fat milk
- 1 large egg
- Powdered sugar and sliced strawberries, for serving

Directions
For the Filling
a) Pour the chocolate chips into a bowl and pour the cream into a small saucepan.
b) Heat the cream until the edges bubble, then pour over the chocolate.
c) Let the chocolate sit for 2 minutes (this helps the chocolate melt), then stir to form a thick ganache.
d) Line a baking sheet with parchment paper.
e) Oil the inside of a 2-inch round cookie cutter.
f) Pour 1 teaspoon of the chocolate into the cookie cutter and spread it out so that it forms a circle. Remove the cutter and continue making ganache circles (should yield about six).
g) Place the baking sheet into the freezer and freeze the ganache for at least 4 hours to overnight.

For the Pancakes
a) Add all items, except the strawberries, to a high-speed blender and blitz on high to liquefy. Make sure everything is well blended.

b) Pour the batter into a bowl and let it rest for 2 to 3 minutes. This allows the batter to thicken up so that it can hold the chocolate when you flip the pancakes.
c) Spray a non-stick skillet or griddle generously with vegetable oil and heat over medium heat.
d) Once the skillet is hot, use a ¼-cup measuring cup to pour the batter into a skillet.
e) Gently spread the batter into a round shape with the measuring cup.
f) Place 1 frozen ganache circle (flipped so that the lumpy side is down) in the center of the batter and gently press it into the batter. Pour more batter over ganache circle just until it is covered.
g) Cook until the batter is dry to the touch (about 3 to 4 minutes), then carefully flip the pancake.
h) Continue cooking until the other side of the pancake is golden brown.
i) Once the pancake is cooked on that side, remove the pancake from the heat and place on a plate.
j) Continue with remaining batter and chocolate.
k) Serve pancakes with powdered sugar and sliced strawberries.

53. Pineapple upside-down pancakes

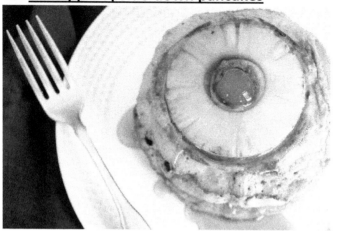

Ingredients:
- 1 (20-ounce) can pineapple rings (drained)
- 1¾ cups old-fashioned rolled oats
- 1½ teaspoons baking powder
- 1 teaspoon baking soda
- ½ teaspoon cinnamon
- ¼ teaspoon salt
- 2 tablespoons maple syrup
- 2 tablespoons coconut oil (melted)
- 1½ cups 2% low-fat milk
- 1 large egg
- Brown sugar
- Maraschino cherries (de-stemmed and cut in half), for serving

Directions

a) Place the pineapple rings on a double layer of paper towels to drain excess liquid.
b) Add all items, except pineapple, brown sugar, and maraschino cherries, to a high-speed blender and blitz on high to liquefy. Make sure everything is well blended.
c) Pour batter into a bowl and let it rest for 2 to 3 minutes. This allows the batter to thicken up so that it can hold those pineapple rings when you flip the pancakes.
d) Spray a non-stick skillet or griddle generously with vegetable oil and heat over medium heat.
e) Once the skillet is hot, use a ¼-cup measuring cup to pour the batter into the pan. Gently spread batter into a round shape with the measuring cup.
f) Place pineapple ring in the center of the batter and gently press it into the batter. Lightly sprinkle some brown sugar directly onto the pineapple ring.
g) Cook until the batter is dry to the touch (about 3 to 4 minutes), then carefully flip the pancake.
h) Continue cooking until the pineapple is good and caramelized.
i) Once the pancake is cooked on that side, remove the pancake from the heat and place on a plate.
j) Serve each pancake with a maraschino cherry placed in the center of the pineapple.

54. Lemon meringue pancakes

Ingredients:
Meringue
- 4 large egg whites
- 3 tablespoons sugar

Pancakes
- 2 eggs
- ½ cup cottage cheese
- ½ teaspoon vanilla extract
- 1 tablespoon honey
- ¼ cup spelt flour
- ½ teaspoon baking powder
- ¼ teaspoon baking soda
- 2 teaspoons sugar-free lemon Jell-O mix

Directions
For the Meringue
a) Add the egg whites to a mixing bowl and beat until soft peaks form. Soft peaks happen when you pull the beaters from the mixture and the peak forms but falls over quickly.
b) Add the sugar to the egg whites and continue to beat until stiff peaks form. Stiff peaks happen when you pull the beaters from the mixture and the peak forms and holds its shape.
c) Set the meringue aside.
d) Whisk the eggs, cottage cheese, vanilla, and honey together and set aside.
e) In another bowl, whisk the dry Ingredients together until well combined.
f) Add the wet Ingredients to the dry Ingredients and whisk until thoroughly combined.
g) Spray a non-stick skillet or griddle generously with vegetable oil and heat over medium heat.
h) Once the skillet is hot, add the batter using a ¼-cup measuring cup and pour the batter into the skillet to make

the pancake. Use the measuring cup to help shape the pancake.

i) Cook until the sides appear set and bubbles form in the middle (about 2 to 3 minutes), then flip the pancake.
j) Once the pancake is cooked on that side, remove pancake from the heat and place on a plate.
k) Continue these steps with the rest of the batter.
l) Top pancakes with the meringue.
m) To toast the meringue you can either use a torch to lightly brown the edges or you can pop the topped pancakes under a hot broiler for 2 to 3 minutes.

55. Cinnamon roll pancakes

Ingredients:
Cashew Cream Cheese Topping
- 1 cup raw cashews
- ⅓ cup water
- 2 tablespoons honey
- 1 teaspoon apple cider vinegar
- 1 teaspoon lemon juice
- ½ teaspoon vanilla extract
- ½ teaspoon kosher salt

Cinnamon Filling
- ½ cup brown sugar
- 4 tablespoons butter, melted
- 3 teaspoons cinnamon

Pancakes
- 1¾ cups old-fashioned rolled oats
- 1½ teaspoons baking powder
- 1 teaspoon baking soda
- ½ teaspoon cinnamon
- ¼ teaspoon salt
- 2 tablespoons coconut oil, melted
- 1 tablespoon maple syrup
- 1 large egg
- 1 teaspoon vanilla extract
- 1½ cups 2% low-fat milk

Directions
a) Soak cashews in water overnight.
b) Drain cashews, then add them to a blender along with the rest of the Ingredients.
c) Blitz the cashew mixture until it's creamy and has no lumps.
d) Scrape the topping into a small-lidded container and set it aside.

For the Cinnamon Filling
a) Add all of the Ingredients together and stir to combine, making sure that you have broken down any lumps.

b) Pour this mixture into a sandwich bag. You're going to cut the corner tip off the bag and use it as a squeeze bag to pipe the cinnamon swirl onto the pancakes.

For the Pancakes

a) Add all of the Ingredients to a blender. The melted coconut oil might harden up when combined with colder Ingredients, so you can slightly warm the milk to help prevent this from happening if you'd like.
b) Blitz everything in the blender until you have a smooth liquid.
c) Pour pancake mixture into a large bowl.
d) Let batter rest for 5 to 10 minutes. This allows all of the Ingredients to come together and gives the batter a better consistency.
e) Spray a non-stick skillet or griddle generously with vegetable oil and heat over medium heat.
f) Once the skillet is hot, add batter using a ¼-cup measuring cup and pour the batter onto the skillet to make the pancake. Gently spread the batter into a round shape with the measuring cup.
g) Cut the tip from the bag of Cinnamon Filling and squeeze a cinnamon swirl onto the pancake.
h) Cook until the sides appear set and bubbles form in the middle (about 2 to 3 minutes), then flip the pancake.
i) Once the pancake is cooked on that side, remove pancake from the heat and place on a plate.
j) Serve pancakes with the Cashew Cream Cheese Topping.

56. Kefir pancakes

Ingredients:
- 1½ cups spelt flour
- 1½ teaspoons baking powder
- 1 teaspoon baking soda
- ½ teaspoon salt
- 2 tablespoons coconut oil, melted
- 2 large eggs, beaten
- ¼ cup 2% low-fat milk
- 1¼ cups plain kefir, slightly warmed
- ¼ cup maple syrup
- Blueberries, for serving (optional)

Directions

a) Add the flour, baking powder, baking soda, and salt in a large bowl and whisk to thoroughly combine.
b) Add the remaining Ingredients to another bowl and whisk to thoroughly combine. The melted coconut oil might harden up when combined with colder Ingredients, so you can slightly warm the milk to help prevent this from happening if you'd like.
c) Pour the wet Ingredients into the dry Ingredients and whisk to combine until all the Ingredients are wet.
d) Let the batter rest for 2 to 3 minutes. This allows all of the Ingredients to come together and gives the batter a better consistency.
e) Spray a non-stick skillet or griddle generously with vegetable oil and heat over medium heat.
f) Once the skillet is hot, add the batter using a ¼-cup measuring cup and pour the batter into the skillet to make the pancake. Use the measuring cup to help shape the pancake.
g) Cook until the sides appear set and bubbles form in the middle (about 2 to 3 minutes), then flip the pancake.
h) Once the pancake is cooked on that side, remove pancake from the heat and place on a plate.
i) Continue these steps with the rest of the batter. Serve with blueberries, if desired.

57. Cottage cheese pancakes

Ingredients:
- ¼ cup spelt flour
- ½ teaspoon baking powder
- ¼ teaspoon baking soda
- ⅛ teaspoon cinnamon
- ⅛ teaspoon salt
- 2 large eggs, beaten
- ½ cup 2% low-fat cottage cheese
- 1 tablespoon honey
- ½ teaspoon vanilla extract
- Strawberries, for serving (optional)

Directions

a) Add all of the dry Ingredients to a bowl and whisk until well combined.
b) In a separate bowl, whisk the wet Ingredients together.
c) Add wet Ingredients to the dry Ingredients and whisk to thoroughly combine them.
d) Let the batter rest for 5 to 10 minutes. This allows all of the Ingredients to come together and gives you a better consistency for the batter.
e) Spray a non-stick skillet or griddle generously with vegetable oil and heat over medium heat.
f) Once the skillet is hot, add the batter using a ¼-cup measuring cup and pour the batter into the skillet to make the pancake. Use the measuring cup to help shape the pancake.
g) Cook until the sides appear set and bubbles form in the middle (about 2 to 3 minutes), then flip the pancake.
h) Once the pancake is cooked on that side, remove pancake from the heat and place on a plate.
i) Continue these steps with the rest of the batter. Serve with strawberries, if desired.

58. Oatmeal pancakes

Ingredients:
- 1¾ cups old-fashioned rolled oats
- 1½ teaspoons baking powder
- 1 teaspoon baking soda
- ½ teaspoon cinnamon
- ¼ teaspoon salt
- 2 tablespoons coconut oil, melted
- 1 tablespoon maple syrup
- 1 large egg
- 1 teaspoon vanilla extract
- 1½ cups 2% low-fat milk
- Strawberries and blueberries, for serving (optional)

Directions

a) Add all of the Ingredients to a blender. The melted coconut oil might harden up when combined with colder Ingredients, so you can slightly warm the milk to help prevent this from happening if you'd like.
b) Blitz everything in the blender until you have a smooth liquid.
c) Pour the pancake mixture into a large bowl.
d) Let batter rest for 5 to 10 minutes. This allows all of the Ingredients to come together and gives the batter a better consistency.
e) Spray a non-stick skillet or griddle generously with vegetable oil and heat over medium heat.
f) Once the skillet is hot, add the batter using a ¼-cup measuring cup and pour the batter into the skillet to make the pancake. Use the measuring cup to help shape the pancake.
g) Cook until the sides appear set and bubbles form in the middle (about 2 to 3 minutes), then flip the pancake.
h) Once the pancake is cooked on that side, remove pancake from the heat and place on a plate.
i) Continue these steps with the rest of the batter. Serve with berries, if desired.

59. 3-Ingredient pancakes

Ingredients:
- 1 ripe banana, plus more for serving
- 2 large eggs
- ½ teaspoon baking powder

Directions

a) Add the banana to a bowl and mash it until it's nice and creamy—no lumps.
b) Crack the eggs into another bowl and whisk until they are thoroughly mixed.
c) Add the baking powder to the bowl of banana and then pour in the eggs. Whisk to completely combine everything together.
d) Spray a non-stick skillet or griddle generously with vegetable oil and heat over medium heat.
e) Once the skillet is hot, add 2 tablespoons of batter into the pan to make the pancake.
f) Cook until the sides appear set (you won't see any bubbles), then carefully flip the pancake.
g) Once the pancake is cooked on that side, remove the pancake from the heat and place on a plate.
h) Continue these steps with the rest of the batter. Serve with sliced banana, if desired.

60. Almond butter pancakes

Ingredients:
- 1 large egg
- 1 tablespoon coconut oil, melted
- 1 tablespoon maple syrup
- 1 tablespoon almond butter, plus more for serving
- 1 teaspoon baking powder
- ½ teaspoon vanilla extract
- ¼ teaspoon salt
- ½ cup 2% low-fat milk
- ¾ cup spelt flour
- Cherries, for serving (optional)

Directions

a) In a large bowl, add the egg, coconut oil, maple syrup, almond butter, baking powder, vanilla, and salt, then whisk to thoroughly combine.
b) Add the milk to the mixture and whisk again to combine.
c) Add the flour to the mixture and whisk to thoroughly combine the Ingredients.
d) Let the batter rest for 2 to 3 minutes. This allows the batter to thicken up so that all the Ingredients come together.
e) Spray a non-stick skillet or griddle generously with vegetable oil and heat over medium heat.
f) Once the skillet is hot, add the batter using a ¼-cup measuring cup and pour the batter into the skillet to make the pancake. Use the measuring cup to help shape the pancake.
g) Cook until the sides appear set and bubbles form in the middle (about 2 to 3 minutes), then flip the pancake.
h) Once the pancake is cooked on that side, remove pancake from the heat and place on a plate.
i) Continue these steps with the rest of the batter.
j) Serve pancakes with melted almond butter and cherries, if desired. To melt almond butter, scoop out desired amount into microwave-safe dish and heat on high in 30-second intervals until melted. Stir between heating.

61. Tiramisu pancakes

Ingredients:
- 1¾ cups old-fashioned rolled oats
- 1½ tablespoons sugar-free vanilla Jell-O pudding mix
- 2 teaspoons instant espresso
- 1½ teaspoons cocoa powder
- 1½ teaspoons baking powder
- 1 teaspoon baking soda
- ½ teaspoon cinnamon
- ¼ teaspoon salt
- 2 tablespoons coconut oil, melted
- 1 tablespoon maple syrup
- 1 large egg
- 1 teaspoon vanilla extract
- 1 cup 2% low-fat milk
- Whipped cream, for serving
- Chocolate shavings, for serving

Directions

a) Add all of the Ingredients, except for the whipped cream and chocolate shavings, to a blender. The melted coconut oil might harden up when combined with colder Ingredients, so you can slightly warm the milk to help prevent this from happening if you'd like.
b) Blitz everything in the blender until you have a smooth liquid.
c) Pour the pancake mixture into a large bowl.
d) Let the batter rest for 2 to 3 minutes. This allows all of the Ingredients to come together and gives the batter a better consistency.
e) Spray a non-stick skillet or griddle generously with vegetable oil and heat over medium heat.
f) Once the skillet is hot, add the batter using a ¼-cup measuring cup and pour the batter into the skillet to make the pancake. Use the measuring cup to help shape the pancake.
g) Cook until the sides appear set and bubbles form in the middle (about 2 to 3 minutes), then flip the pancake.
h) Once the pancake is cooked on that side, remove pancake from the heat and place on a plate.
i) Continue these steps with the rest of the batter.
j) Top with whipped cream and chocolate shavings.

62. Lemon blueberry pancakes

Ingredients:
- 1½ cups spelt flour
- 1½ teaspoons baking powder
- 1 teaspoon baking soda
- ½ teaspoon salt
- Zest from 1 lemon
- 2 tablespoons coconut oil, melted
- 2 large eggs, beaten
- ¼ cup 2% low-fat milk
- ¼ cup maple syrup, plus more for serving
- 1¼ cups plain kefir (slightly warmed)
- ½ cup blueberries

Directions

a) Add the flour, baking powder, baking soda, and salt to a large bowl and whisk to thoroughly combine.
b) Add the coconut oil, eggs, milk, maple syrup, lemon zest, and kefir to a bowl and whisk to combine. The melted coconut oil might harden up when combined with colder Ingredients, so you can slightly warm the kefir to help prevent this from happening if you'd like.
c) Pour the wet Ingredients into the dry Ingredients and whisk to combine until all the Ingredients are wet.
d) Let the batter rest for 2 to 3 minutes. This allows all of the Ingredients to come together and gives the batter a better consistency.
e) Spray a non-stick skillet or griddle generously with vegetable oil and heat over medium heat.
f) Once the skillet is hot, add the batter using a ¼-cup measuring cup and pour the batter into the skillet to make the pancake. Use the measuring cup to help shape the pancake.
g) Place 3 to 5 blueberries onto each pancake. Keep the berries toward the center so it's easier to flip the pancake.
h) Cook until the sides appear set and bubbles form in the middle (about 2 to 3 minutes), then flip the pancake.
i) Once the pancake is cooked on that side, remove pancake from the heat and place on a plate.
j) Continue these steps with the rest of the batter. Serve with maple syrup.

63. <u>Quinoa pancakes</u>

Ingredients:
- 1 cup (any color) cooked quinoa
- ¾ cup quinoa flour
- 2 teaspoons baking powder
- ½ teaspoon salt
- 1 tablespoon melted butter
- ¼ cup Greek yogurt
- 2 tablespoons 2% low-fat milk
- 2 large eggs, beaten
- 2 tablespoons maple syrup
- 1 teaspoon vanilla extract
- Fruit preserves, for serving (optional)

a) In a large bowl, add the quinoa, flour, baking powder, and salt together and whisk to thoroughly combine.
b) In another bowl, whisk butter, yogurt, milk, eggs, maple syrup, and vanilla. Whisk everything together so that it is well combined.
c) Add the wet Ingredients to the dry Ingredients and whisk until thoroughly combined.
d) Let the batter rest for 2 to 3 minutes. This allows all of the Ingredients to come together and gives the batter a better consistency.
e) Spray a non-stick skillet or griddle generously with vegetable oil and heat over medium heat.
f) Once the skillet is hot, add the batter using a ¼-cup measuring cup and pour the batter into the skillet to make the pancake. Use the measuring cup to help shape the pancake.
g) Cook until the sides appear set and bubbles form in the middle (about 2 to 3 minutes), then flip the pancake.
h) Once the pancake is cooked on that side, remove pancake from the heat and place on a plate.
i) Continue these steps with the rest of the batter. Serve with fruit preserves, if desired.

64. <u>**Greek yogurt oatmeal pancakes**</u>

Ingredients:
- 1¾ cups old-fashioned rolled oats
- 1½ teaspoons baking powder
- 1 teaspoon baking soda
- ½ teaspoon cinnamon
- ¼ teaspoon salt
- 1 large egg
- 2 tablespoons coconut oil, melted
- 1 tablespoon maple syrup, plus more to serve
- 1 teaspoon vanilla extract
- 1 cup plain Greek yogurt
- ¼ cup 2% low-fat milk

Directions

a) Add all of the Ingredients to a blender. The melted coconut oil might harden up when combined with colder Ingredients, so you can slightly warm the milk to help prevent this from happening if you'd like.
b) Blitz everything in the blender until you have a smooth liquid.
c) Pour the pancake mixture into a large bowl.
d) Let the batter rest for 5 to 10 minutes. This allows all of the Ingredients to come together and gives the batter a better consistency.
e) Spray a non-stick skillet or griddle generously with vegetable oil and heat over medium heat.
f) Once the skillet is hot, add the batter using a ¼-cup measuring cup and pour the batter into the skillet to make the pancake. Use the measuring cup to help shape the pancake.
g) Cook until the sides appear set and bubbles form in the middle (about 2 minutes), then flip the pancake.
h) Once the pancake is cooked on that side, remove pancake from the heat and place on a plate.
i) Continue these steps with the rest of the batter. Serve with maple syrup.

65. Gingerbread pancakes

Ingredients:
Topping
- ¼ cup plain Greek yogurt
- 1 tablespoon maple syrup

Pancakes
- 1 cup spelt flour
- 1 teaspoon baking soda
- 1 teaspoon ground ginger
- 1 teaspoon ground allspice
- 1 teaspoon cinnamon
- ¼ teaspoon ground cloves
- ¼ teaspoon salt
- 1 large egg
- ½ cup 2% low-fat milk
- 3 tablespoons maple syrup
- 1 teaspoon vanilla extract

Directions

a) Mix the Greek yogurt and maple syrup together until well combined and set aside.
b) In a large bowl, add the spelt flour, baking soda, ginger, allspice, cinnamon, cloves, and salt together and whisk to thoroughly combine.
c) In another bowl, whisk the egg, milk, maple syrup, and vanilla together until well combined.
d) Add the wet Ingredients to the dry Ingredients and whisk until thoroughly combined.
e) Let the batter rest for 2 to 3 minutes. This allows all of the Ingredients to come together and gives the batter a better consistency.
f) Spray a non-stick skillet or griddle generously with vegetable oil and heat over medium heat.
g) Once the skillet is hot, add the batter using a ¼-cup measuring cup and pour the batter into the skillet to make the pancake.
h) Cook until the sides appear set and bubbles form in the middle.
i) Once the pancake is cooked on that side, remove pancake from the heat and place on a plate.
j) Continue these steps with the rest of the batter. Serve with yogurt topping.

66. Greek yogurt pancakes

Ingredients:
- 1 cup spelt flour
- ½ teaspoon baking powder
- ½ teaspoon baking soda
- ¾ cup plain Greek yogurt
- ½ cup + 2 tablespoons 2% low-fat milk
- 1 large egg
- 2 tablespoons maple syrup

Directions

a) Add the flour, baking powder, and baking soda to a bowl and whisk to combine.
b) In another bowl, whisk the yogurt, milk, egg, and maple syrup together until thoroughly combined.
c) Add the wet Ingredients to the dry Ingredients and whisk until thoroughly combined.
d) Let the batter rest for 2 to 3 minutes. This allows all of the Ingredients to come together and gives the batter a better consistency.
e) Spray a non-stick skillet or griddle generously with vegetable oil and heat over medium heat.
f) Once the skillet is hot, add the batter using a ¼-cup measuring cup and pour the batter into the skillet to make the pancake. Use the measuring cup to help shape the pancake.
g) Cook until the sides appear set and bubbles form in the middle (about 2 to 3 minutes), then flip the pancake.
h) Once the pancake is cooked on that side, remove pancake from the heat and place on a plate.
i) Continue these steps with the rest of the batter.

67. Oatmeal raisin cookie pancakes

Ingredients:
Topping
- ½ cup powdered sugar
- 1 tablespoon 2% low-fat milk

Pancakes
- 1¾ cups old-fashioned rolled oats
- 2 tablespoons brown sugar
- 1½ teaspoons baking powder
- 1 teaspoon baking soda
- ½ teaspoon cinnamon
- ¼ teaspoon salt
- 2 tablespoons coconut oil, melted
- 1 teaspoon vanilla extract
- 1 cup 2% low-fat milk
- ⅓ cup chopped golden raisins

Directions
For the Topping

a) In a small bowl, mix the powdered sugar and milk together until it's smooth. Set aside.
b) For the Pancakes
c) Add all of the Ingredients, except for the raisins, to the blender. The melted coconut oil might harden up when combined with colder Ingredients, so you can slightly warm the milk to help prevent this from happening if you'd like.
d) Blitz everything in the blender until you have a smooth liquid.
e) Pour the pancake mixture into a large bowl.
f) Stir in the chopped raisins.
g) Let the batter rest for 5 to 10 minutes. This allows all of the Ingredients to come together and gives the batter a better consistency.
h) Spray a non-stick skillet or griddle generously with vegetable oil and heat over medium heat.

i) Once the skillet is hot, add the batter using a ¼-cup measuring cup and pour the batter into the skillet to make the pancake. Use the measuring cup to help shape the pancake.
j) Cook until the sides appear set and bubbles form in the middle (about 2 to 3 minutes), then flip the pancake.
k) Once the pancake is cooked on that side, remove pancake from the heat and place on a plate.
l) Continue these steps with the rest of the batter.
m) Top with sugar topping.

68. Peanut butter and jelly pancakes

Ingredients:
- 1½ cups spelt flour
- ¾ cup powdered peanut butter
- 1½ teaspoons baking powder
- 1 teaspoon baking soda
- ½ teaspoon salt
- 2 large eggs, beaten
- 1 tablespoon butter, melted
- 1½ cups 2% low-fat milk
- Concord grape jelly, for serving

Directions

a) Add flour, powdered peanut butter, baking powder, baking soda, and salt to a bowl and whisk to combine.
b) In another bowl, whisk the eggs, butter, and milk together until thoroughly combined.
c) Add the wet Ingredients to the dry Ingredients and whisk until thoroughly combined.
d) Let the batter rest for 2 to 3 minutes. This allows all of the Ingredients to come together and gives the batter a better consistency.
e) Spray a non-stick skillet or griddle generously with vegetable oil and heat over medium heat.
f) Once the skillet is hot, add the batter using a ¼-cup measuring cup and pour the batter into the skillet to make the pancake. Use the measuring cup to help shape the pancake.
g) Cook until the sides appear set and bubbles form in the middle (about 2 to 3 minutes), then flip the pancake.
h) Once the pancake is cooked on that side, remove pancake from the heat and place on a plate.
i) Continue these steps with the rest of the batter. Top with the grape jelly.

69. **Bacon pancakes**

Ingredients:
- 8 slices center-cut bacon
- 1½ cups spelt flour
- 1½ teaspoons baking powder
- 1 teaspoon baking soda
- ½ teaspoon salt
- 2 large eggs, beaten
- 1 tablespoon butter, melted
- 1 teaspoon vanilla extract
- 1¼ cups 2% low-fat milk
- ¼ cup maple syrup

Directions

a) Preheat the oven to 350°F.
b) Arrange the bacon, in a single layer, on a rimmed baking sheet lined with parchment paper. This makes cleanup a whole lot easier.
c) Slide the bacon into the oven and cook for 30 minutes, or until the bacon is done.
d) Remove the bacon from the oven and place the bacon on a paper towel-lined plate to cool.
e) In a large bowl, add the flour, baking powder, baking soda, and salt. Whisk to combine Ingredients.
f) In another bowl, add the eggs, butter, vanilla, milk, and maple syrup and whisk to combine Ingredients.
g) Add the wet Ingredients to the dry Ingredients and whisk to thoroughly combine everything.
h) Let the batter rest for 2 to 3 minutes. This allows all of the Ingredients to come together and gives the batter a better consistency.
i) Spray a non-stick skillet or griddle generously with vegetable oil and heat over medium heat.
j) Once the skillet is hot, place a bacon strip onto the skillet. Pour ¼ cup of batter on top of the bacon. Spread the batter evenly over the bacon, as well as the sides of the bacon.
k) Cook until the sides appear set, then flip the pancake over to cook. You may notice that these pancakes cook a little quicker on the bacon side.
l) Once the pancake is cooked on that side, remove the pancake from the heat and place on a plate.
m) Continue these steps with the rest of the batter.

70. Raspberry almond pancakes

Ingredients:
- 1½ cups frozen raspberries, thawed
- 2 tablespoons honey
- 1½ cups almond flour
- 1 teaspoon baking powder
- ¼ teaspoon salt
- ¼ teaspoon cinnamon
- 2 large eggs, beaten
- ¼ cup 2% low-fat milk
- 1 tablespoon maple syrup
- 1 teaspoon vanilla extract

Directions

a) Mix the raspberries with the honey. While mixing the fruit, also smash it to extract more liquid.
b) Pour the Raspberry Topping into a sandwich bag, seal, and set aside.
c) For the Pancakes
d) Add the flour, baking powder, salt, and cinnamon to a bowl and whisk to thoroughly combine.
e) In a separate bowl, whisk the remaining Ingredients together.
f) Add the wet Ingredients to the dry Ingredients and whisk to thoroughly combine them.
g) Let the batter rest for 5 to 10 minutes. This allows all of the Ingredients to come together and gives the batter a better consistency.
h) Spray a non-stick skillet or griddle generously with vegetable oil and heat over medium-high heat.
i) Once the skillet is hot, add batter using a ¼-cup measuring cup and pour the batter into the skillet to make the pancake. Gently spread the batter into a round shape with the measuring cup.
j) Snip one corner of the bag containing the Raspberry Topping and drizzle some of it over the top of the pancake. Use a toothpick to drag the raspberries through the pancake base.
k) Cook until the sides appear set and bubbles form in the middle (about 2 to 3 minutes), then flip the pancake.
l) Once the pancake is cooked on that side, remove pancake from the heat and place on a plate.
m) Continue these steps with the rest of the batter.
n) Top with the remaining raspberry topping.

71. Peanut, banana & chocolate pancakes

Ingredients:
- 1 cup spelt flour
- ¼ cup powdered peanut butter
- ½ teaspoon baking powder
- ½ teaspoon baking soda
- ¾ cup plain Greek yogurt
- 1 ripe medium banana, mashed, plus more for serving (optional)
- ¼ cup + 2 tablespoons 2% low-fat milk
- 1 large egg
- 2 tablespoons maple syrup
- ½ cup chocolate chips, plus more for serving (optional)
- Peanut butter, for serving (optional)

Directions

a) Add the flour, powdered peanut butter, baking powder, and baking soda to a bowl and whisk to combine.
b) In another bowl, whisk the yogurt, mashed banana, milk, egg, and maple syrup until combined.
c) Add the wet Ingredients to the dry Ingredients and whisk until thoroughly combined.
d) Stir in the chocolate chips.
e) Let the batter rest for 2 to 3 minutes. This allows all of the Ingredients to come together and gives the batter a better consistency.
f) Spray a non-stick skillet or griddle generously with vegetable oil and heat over medium heat.
g) Once the skillet is hot, add the batter using a ¼-cup measuring cup and pour the batter into the skillet to make the pancake. Use the measuring cup to help shape the pancake.
h) Cook until the sides appear set and bubbles form in the middle (about 2 to 3 minutes), then flip the pancake.
i) Once the pancake is cooked on that side, remove pancake from the heat and place on a plate.
j) Continue these steps with the rest of the batter.

72. Vanilla coconut pancakes

Ingredients:
Vanilla Coconut Topping
- 1 cup canned full-fat coconut milk
- ¼ cup maple syrup
- 1½ teaspoons vanilla extract
- Small pinch salt

Pancakes
- 1½ cups spelt flour
- ¼ cup shredded unsweetened coconut, toasted (plus more for serving)
- 1½ teaspoons baking powder
- 1 teaspoon baking soda
- ½ teaspoon salt
- 2 large eggs, beaten
- 2 tablespoons coconut oil, melted
- 1 tablespoon vanilla extract
- ¼ cup maple syrup
- ¼ cup canned full-fat coconut milk
- 1¼ cups plain kefir

Directions
a) Add all the Ingredients to a small saucepan and heat over medium heat.
b) Whisk occasionally and cook until the mixture begins to thicken (approximately 7 minutes).
c) Remove from the heat to let it cool slightly.
d) For the Pancakes
e) In a large bowl, add the flour, coconut, baking powder, baking soda, and salt. Whisk to combine Ingredients.
f) In another bowl, add the eggs, coconut oil, vanilla, maple syrup, coconut milk, and kefir and whisk to combine Ingredients. The melted coconut oil might harden up when combined with colder Ingredients, so you can slightly warm the kefir to help prevent this from happening if you'd like.

g) Add the wet Ingredients to the dry Ingredients and whisk to thoroughly combine everything.
h) Let the batter rest for 2 to 3 minutes. This allows all of the Ingredients to come together and gives the batter a better consistency.
i) Spray a non-stick skillet or griddle generously with vegetable oil and heat over medium heat.
j) Once the skillet is hot, add the batter using a ¼-cup measuring cup and pour the batter into the skillet to make the pancake. Use the measuring cup to help shape the pancake.
k) Cook until the sides appear set and bubbles form in the middle (about 2 to 3 minutes), then flip the pancake.
l) Once the pancake is cooked on that side, remove pancake from the heat and place on a plate.
m) Continue these steps with the rest of the batter.
n) Spoon the Vanilla Coconut Topping over the pancakes and sprinkle with the toasted coconut before serving.

73. Chocolate coconut almond pancakes

Ingredients:
- 1½ cups almond flour
- ½ cup shredded, unsweetened coconut, toasted
- 1 teaspoon baking powder
- 1 teaspoon baking soda
- ¼ teaspoon salt
- 2 large eggs, beaten
- ½ cup canned full-fat coconut milk
- 1 tablespoon maple syrup, plus more for serving
- 1 teaspoon vanilla extract
- ½ cup chocolate chips
- Toasted coconut, roasted almonds, and shaved chocolate, for serving

Directions

a) Add the flour, shredded coconut, baking powder, baking soda, and salt to a bowl and whisk to thoroughly combine.
b) In a separate bowl, whisk the eggs, coconut milk, maple syrup, and vanilla together.
c) Add the wet Ingredients to the dry Ingredients and whisk to thoroughly combine them.
d) Stir in the chocolate chips.
e) Let the batter rest for 5 to 10 minutes. This allows all of the Ingredients to come together and gives the batter a better consistency.
f) Spray a non-stick skillet or griddle generously with vegetable oil and heat over medium heat.
g) Once the skillet is hot, add the batter using a ¼-cup measuring cup and pour the batter into the skillet to make the pancake. Use the measuring cup to help shape the pancake.
h) Cook until the sides appear set and bubbles form in the middle (about 2 to 3 minutes), then flip the pancake.
i) Once the pancake is cooked on that side, remove pancake from the heat and place on a plate.
j) Continue these steps with the rest of the batter.
k) Top with toasted coconut, roasted almonds, shredded chocolate, and a drizzle more of maple syrup, if you'd like.

74. Strawberry shortcake pancakes

Ingredients:
- 1¾ cups old-fashioned rolled oats
- 1½ teaspoons baking powder
- 1 teaspoon baking soda
- ½ teaspoon cinnamon
- ¼ teaspoon salt
- 2 tablespoons coconut oil, melted
- 1 tablespoon maple syrup
- 1 large egg
- 1 teaspoon vanilla extract
- 1½ cups 2% low-fat milk
- 1 cup thinly sliced strawberries
- Whipped cream and strawberries, to serve

Directions

a) Add all of the Ingredients, except for the strawberries, to a blender. The melted coconut oil might harden up when combined with colder Ingredients, so you can slightly warm the milk to help prevent this from happening if you'd like.
b) Blitz everything in the blender until you have a smooth liquid.
c) Pour the pancake mixture into a large bowl.
d) Let the batter rest for 5 to 10 minutes. This allows all of the Ingredients to come together and gives the batter a better consistency.
e) Spray a non-stick skillet or griddle generously with vegetable oil and heat over medium heat.
f) Once the skillet is hot, add the batter using a ¼-cup measuring cup and pour the batter into the skillet to make the pancake. Use the measuring cup to help shape the pancake. Place the sliced strawberries in a single layer in the batter.
g) Cook until the sides appear set and bubbles form in the middle (about 2 minutes), then flip the pancake. You may need to let these cook a little longer on the first side so that they don't fall apart when you flip them. The strawberries are heavy and can cause these pancakes to break if they're not completely set on the first side.
h) Once the pancake is cooked on that side, remove pancake from the heat and place on a plate.
i) Continue these steps with the rest of the batter.
j) To serve, layer pancakes with whipped cream and top with strawberries.

75. Peanut butter cup pancakes

Ingredients:
- 1¾ cups old-fashioned rolled oats
- ¼ cup powdered peanut butter
- 1½ teaspoons baking powder
- 1 teaspoon baking soda
- ½ teaspoon cinnamon
- ¼ teaspoon salt
- 2 tablespoons coconut oil, melted
- 1 tablespoon maple syrup
- 1 large egg
- 1 teaspoon vanilla extract
- 1½ cups 2% low-fat milk
- ½ cup chocolate chips

Directions

a) Add all of the Ingredients, except for the chocolate chips, to a blender. The melted coconut oil might harden up when combined with colder Ingredients, so you can slightly warm the milk to help prevent this from happening if you'd like.
b) Blitz everything in the blender until you have a smooth liquid.
c) Pour the pancake batter into a large bowl.
d) Stir in the chocolate chips.
e) Let the batter rest for 5 to 10 minutes. This allows all of the Ingredients to come together and gives the batter a better consistency.
f) Spray a non-stick skillet or griddle generously with vegetable oil and heat over medium heat.
g) Once the skillet is hot, add the batter using a ¼-cup measuring cup and pour the batter into the skillet to make the pancake. Use the measuring cup to help shape the pancake.
h) Cook until the sides appear set and bubbles form in the middle (about 2 to 3 minutes), then flip the pancake.
i) Once the pancake is cooked on that side, remove pancake from the heat and place on a plate.
j) Continue these steps with the rest of the batter.

76. **Mexican chocolate pancakes**

Ingredients:
- 1 cup spelt flour
- ¼ cup unsweetened cocoa
- 1 teaspoon cinnamon
- ½ teaspoon baking powder
- ½ teaspoon baking soda
- ¾ cup plain Greek yogurt
- ¼ cup + 2 tablespoons 2% low-fat milk
- 1 large egg
- 2 tablespoons maple syrup

Directions

a) Add the flour, cocoa, cinnamon, baking powder, and baking soda to a bowl and whisk to combine.
b) In another bowl, whisk the yogurt, milk, egg, and maple syrup together until thoroughly combined.
c) Add the wet Ingredients to the dry Ingredients and whisk until thoroughly combined.
d) Let the batter rest for 2 to 3 minutes. This allows all of the Ingredients to come together and gives the batter a better consistency.
e) Spray a non-stick skillet or griddle generously with vegetable oil and heat over medium heat.
f) Once the skillet is hot, add the batter using a ¼-cup measuring cup and pour the batter into the skillet to make the pancake. Use the measuring cup to help shape the pancake.
g) Cook until the sides appear set and bubbles form in the middle (about 2 to 3 minutes), then flip the pancake.
h) Once the pancake is cooked on that side, remove pancake from the heat and place on a plate.
i) Continue these steps with the rest of the batter.

77. Birthday surprise pancakes

Ingredients:
- 1 cup spelt flour
- 2 tablespoons sugar-free vanilla pudding mix
- ½ teaspoon baking powder
- ½ teaspoon baking soda
- ¾ cup plain Greek yogurt
- ½ cup + 2 tablespoons 2% low-fat milk
- 1 large egg
- 2 tablespoons maple syrup
- ¼ cup rainbow sprinkles, plus more for topping (optional)

Directions

a) Add the flour, pudding, baking powder, and baking soda to a bowl and whisk to combine.
b) In another bowl, whisk the yogurt, milk, egg, and maple syrup together until thoroughly combined.
c) Add the wet Ingredients to the dry Ingredients and whisk until thoroughly combined.
d) Let the batter rest for 2 to 3 minutes. This allows all of the Ingredients to come together and gives the batter a better consistency.
e) After the batter rests, stir in the sprinkles.
f) Spray a non-stick skillet or griddle generously with vegetable oil and heat over medium heat.
g) Once the skillet is hot, add the batter using a ¼-cup measuring cup and pour the batter into the skillet to make the pancake. Use the measuring cup to help shape the pancake.
h) Cook until the sides appear set and bubbles form in the middle (about 2 to 3 minutes), then flip the pancake.
i) Once the pancake is cooked on that side, remove pancake from the heat and place on a plate.
j) Continue these steps with the rest of the batter.

78. Green monster pancakes

Ingredients:
- 1½ cups spelt flour
- 2 tablespoons hemp powder
- 1 tablespoon spirulina powder
- 1½ teaspoons baking powder
- 1 teaspoon baking soda
- ½ teaspoon salt
- 2 tablespoons coconut oil, melted
- 1½ tablespoons honey
- 1 tablespoon vanilla extract
- 2 large eggs, beaten
- ¼ cup canned full-fat coconut milk
- 1¼ cups plain kefir (slightly warmed)

Directions

a) Add the spelt flour, hemp powder, spirulina powder, baking powder, baking soda, and salt to a bowl and whisk to combine.
b) In another bowl, whisk the coconut oil, honey, vanilla, eggs, coconut milk, and kefir together until they are well combined. The melted coconut oil might harden up when combined with colder Ingredients, so you can slightly warm the kefir to help prevent this from happening if you'd like.
c) Add the wet Ingredients to the dry Ingredients and whisk together until thoroughly combined.
d) Let the batter rest for 2 to 3 minutes. This allows all of the Ingredients to come together and gives the batter a better consistency.
e) Spray a non-stick skillet or griddle generously with vegetable oil and heat over medium heat.
f) Once the skillet is hot, add the batter using a ¼-cup measuring cup and pour the batter into the skillet to make the pancake. Use the measuring cup to help shape the pancake.
g) Cook until the sides appear set and bubbles form in the middle (about 2 to 3 minutes), then flip the pancake.
h) Once the pancake is cooked on that side, remove pancake from the heat and place on a plate.
i) Continue these steps with the rest of the batter.

79. Vanilla matcha pancakes

Ingredients:
- 1¾ cups old-fashioned rolled oats
- 2 tablespoons unsweetened matcha powder
- 2 tablespoons sugar-free vanilla pudding mix
- 1½ teaspoons baking powder
- 1 teaspoon baking soda
- ¼ teaspoon salt
- 2 tablespoons coconut oil, melted
- 1 tablespoon maple syrup
- 1 large egg
- 1 teaspoon vanilla extract
- 1½ cups 2% low-fat milk

Directions

a) Add all of the Ingredients to a blender. The melted coconut oil might harden up when combined with colder Ingredients, so you can slightly warm the milk to help prevent this from happening if you'd like.
b) Blitz everything in the blender until you have a smooth liquid.
c) Pour the pancake mixture into a large bowl.
d) Let the batter rest for 5 to 10 minutes. This allows all of the Ingredients to come together and gives the batter a better consistency.
e) Spray a non-stick skillet or griddle generously with vegetable oil and heat over medium heat.
f) Once the skillet is hot, add the batter using a ¼-cup measuring cup and pour the batter into the skillet to make the pancake. Use the measuring cup to help shape the pancake.
g) Cook until the sides appear set and bubbles form in the middle (about 2 to 3 minutes), then flip the pancake.
h) Once the pancake is cooked on that side, remove pancake from the heat and place on a plate.
i) Continue these steps with the rest of the batter.

80. Piña colada pancakes

Ingredients:
- 1 cup spelt flour
- ½ teaspoon baking powder
- ½ teaspoon baking soda
- ¾ cup plain Greek yogurt
- ½ cup + 2 tablespoons canned full-fat coconut milk
- 1 large egg
- 2 tablespoons maple syrup
- 1 teaspoon vanilla extract
- ½ cup finely diced pineapple

Directions

a) Add the flour, baking powder, and baking soda to a bowl and whisk to combine.
b) In another bowl, whisk the yogurt, coconut milk, egg, maple syrup, and vanilla together until thoroughly combined.
c) Add the wet Ingredients to the dry Ingredients and whisk together until thoroughly combined.
d) Once everything is mixed together, stir in the pineapple.
e) Let the batter rest for 2 to 3 minutes. This allows all of the Ingredients to come together and gives the batter a better consistency.
f) Spray a non-stick skillet or griddle generously with vegetable oil and heat over medium heat.
g) Once the skillet is hot, add the batter using a ¼-cup measuring cup and pour the batter into the skillet to make the pancake. Use the measuring cup to help shape the pancake.
h) Cook until the sides appear set and bubbles form in the middle (about 2 to 3 minutes), then flip the pancake.
i) Once the pancake is cooked on that side, remove pancake from the heat and place on a plate.
j) Continue these steps with the rest of the batter.

81. Cherry almond pancakes

Ingredients:
- 1½ cups almond flour
- 1 teaspoon baking powder
- 1 teaspoon baking soda
- ¼ teaspoon salt
- 2 large eggs, beaten
- 1 tablespoon maple syrup
- 1 teaspoon vanilla extract
- ½ cup canned full-fat coconut milk
- ½ cup finely diced sweet cherries
- ¼ cup sliced almonds

Directions

a) Add the flour, baking powder, baking soda, and salt to a bowl and whisk to thoroughly combine.
b) In a separate bowl, whisk the eggs, maple syrup, vanilla, and coconut milk together.
c) Add the wet Ingredients to the dry Ingredients and whisk to thoroughly combine them.
d) Now whisk in the cherries and almonds and mix until everything is well blended.
e) Let the batter rest for 5 to 10 minutes. This allows all of the Ingredients to come together and gives the batter a better consistency.
f) Spray a non-stick skillet or griddle generously with vegetable oil and heat over medium-high heat.
g) Once the skillet is hot, add the batter using a ¼-cup measuring cup and pour the batter into the skillet to make the pancake. Use the measuring cup to help shape the pancake.
h) Cook until the sides appear set and bubbles form in the middle (about 2 to 3 minutes), then flip the pancake.
i) Once the pancake is cooked on that side, remove pancake from the heat and place on a plate.
j) Continue these steps with the rest of the batter.

82. Key lime pancakes

Ingredients:
- 2 eggs
- ½ cup cottage cheese
- ½ teaspoon vanilla extract
- 1 tablespoon honey
- Zest from 1 lime
- ¼ cup spelt flour
- ½ teaspoon baking powder
- ¼ teaspoon baking soda
- 2 teaspoons sugar-free lime Jell-O mix

Directions

a) Whisk the eggs, cottage cheese, vanilla, honey, and lime zest together and set aside.
b) In another bowl, whisk the remaining Ingredients together until well combined.
c) Add the wet Ingredients to the dry Ingredients and whisk until thoroughly combined.
d) Spray a non-stick skillet or griddle generously with vegetable oil and heat over medium heat.
e) Once the skillet is hot, add the batter using a ¼-cup measuring cup and pour the batter into the skillet to make the pancake. Use the measuring cup to help shape the pancake.
f) Cook until the sides appear set and bubbles form in the middle (about 2 to 3 minutes), then flip the pancake.
g) Once the pancake is cooked on that side, remove pancake from the heat and place on a plate.
h) Continue these steps with the rest of the batter.

83. Pumpkin spice pancakes

Ingredients:
- 1½ cups old-fashioned rolled oats
- 1½ teaspoons baking powder
- ½ teaspoon baking soda
- ½ teaspoon cinnamon
- ½ teaspoon ground allspice
- ½ teaspoon ground ginger
- ¼ teaspoon salt
- ½ cup canned pumpkin
- 2 tablespoons coconut oil, melted
- 2 tablespoons maple syrup
- 1 large egg
- 1 teaspoon vanilla extract
- 1 cup 2% low-fat milk

Directions

a) Add all of the Ingredients to a blender. The melted coconut oil might harden up when combined with colder Ingredients, so you can slightly warm the milk to help prevent this from happening if you'd like.
b) Blitz everything in the blender until you have a smooth liquid.
c) Pour the pancake mixture into a large bowl.
d) Let the batter rest for 5 to 10 minutes. This allows all of the Ingredients to come together and gives the batter a better consistency.
e) Spray a non-stick skillet or griddle generously with vegetable oil and heat over medium heat.
f) Once the skillet is hot, add the batter using a ¼-cup measuring cup and pour the batter into the skillet to make the pancake. Use the measuring cup to help shape the pancake.
g) Cook until the sides appear set and bubbles form in the middle (about 2 to 3 minutes), then flip the pancake.
h) Once the pancake is cooked on that side, remove pancake from the heat and place on a plate.
i) Continue these steps with the rest of the batter.

84. Chocolate banana pancakes

Ingredients:
- 1 ripe banana, plus more to serve
- 2 large eggs
- ½ teaspoon baking powder
- 2 tablespoons unsweetened cocoa powder
- Maple syrup, to serve

Directions

a) Add the banana to a bowl and mash it until it's nice and creamy—no lumps.
b) Crack the eggs into another bowl and whisk until they are thoroughly mixed.
c) Add the baking powder and cocoa powder to the bowl of banana and then pour in the eggs. Whisk to completely combine everything together.
d) Spray a non-stick skillet or griddle generously with vegetable oil and heat over medium heat.
e) Once the skillet is hot, add 2 tablespoons of batter into the pan to make the pancake.
f) Cook until the sides appear set (you won't see any bubbles), then carefully flip the pancake.
g) Once the pancake is cooked on that side, remove the pancake from the heat and place on a plate.
h) Continue these steps with the rest of the batter. Serve with sliced banana and maple syrup, if desired.

85. Vanilla almond pancakes

Ingredients:
- 1 cup spelt flour
- 2 tablespoons sugar-free vanilla pudding mix
- ½ teaspoon baking powder
- ½ teaspoon baking soda
- ¾ cup plain Greek yogurt
- ½ cup + 2 tablespoons 2% low-fat milk
- 1 large egg
- 2 tablespoons maple syrup
- ¼ cup sliced almonds

Directions

a) Add the flour, pudding mix, baking powder, and baking soda to a bowl and whisk to combine.
b) In another bowl, whisk the yogurt, milk, egg, and maple syrup together until thoroughly combined.
c) Add the wet Ingredients to the dry Ingredients and whisk until thoroughly combined.
d) Stir in the almonds last.
e) Let the batter rest for 2 to 3 minutes. This allows all of the Ingredients to come together and gives the batter a better consistency.
f) Spray a non-stick skillet or griddle generously with vegetable oil and heat over medium heat.
g) Once the skillet is hot, add the batter using a ¼-cup measuring cup and pour the batter into the skillet to make the pancake. Use the measuring cup to help shape the pancake.
h) Cook until the sides appear set and bubbles form in the middle (about 2 to 3 minutes), then flip the pancake.
i) Once the pancake is cooked on that side, remove pancake from the heat and place on a plate.
j) Continue these steps with the rest of the batter.

86. Funky monkey pancakes

Ingredients:
- 1½ cups almond flour
- 1 teaspoon baking powder
- 1 teaspoon baking soda
- ¼ teaspoon salt
- 1 ripe medium banana, mashed, plus more to serve
- 2 large eggs, beaten
- ½ cup coconut milk
- 1 tablespoon maple syrup
- 1 teaspoon vanilla extract
- ½ cup chopped walnuts
- ½ cup dark chocolate chips, plus more to serve

Directions

a) Add the flour, baking powder, baking soda, and salt to a bowl and whisk to thoroughly combine.
b) In a separate bowl, whisk the mashed banana, eggs, coconut milk, maple syrup, and vanilla together.
c) Add the wet Ingredients to the dry Ingredients and whisk to thoroughly combine them.
d) Now whisk in the walnuts and chocolate chips and mix until everything is well blended.
e) Let the batter rest for 5 to 10 minutes. This allows all of the Ingredients to come together and gives the batter a better consistency.
f) Spray a non-stick skillet or griddle generously with vegetable oil and heat over medium-high heat.
g) Once the skillet is hot, add the batter using a ¼-cup measuring cup and pour the batter into the skillet to make the pancake. Use the measuring cup to help shape the pancake.
h) Cook until the sides appear set and bubbles form in the middle, then flip the pancake.
i) Once the pancake is cooked on that side, remove pancake from the heat and place on a plate.
j) Serve with sliced bananas and chocolate chips.

87. Vanilla pancakes

Ingredients:
- 1½ cups spelt flour
- 2 tablespoons sugar-free vanilla pudding mix
- 1½ teaspoons baking powder
- 1 teaspoon baking soda
- ½ teaspoon salt
- 2 large eggs, beaten
- 2 tablespoons coconut oil, melted
- 1 tablespoon vanilla extract
- ¼ cup maple syrup, plus more for serving
- 1¼ cups plain kefir

Directions

a) Add the spelt flour, pudding mix, baking powder, baking soda, and salt to a bowl and whisk to combine.
b) In another bowl, whisk the eggs, coconut oil, vanilla, maple syrup, and kefir together until they are well combined. The melted coconut oil might harden up when combined with colder Ingredients, so you can slightly warm the kefir to help prevent this from happening if you'd like.
c) Add the wet Ingredients to the dry Ingredients and whisk until thoroughly combined.
d) Let the batter rest for 2 to 3 minutes. This allows all of the Ingredients to come together and gives the batter a better consistency.
e) Spray a non-stick skillet or griddle generously with vegetable oil and heat over medium heat.
f) Once the skillet is hot, add the batter using a ¼-cup measuring cup and pour the batter into the skillet to make the pancake. Use the measuring cup to help shape the pancake.
g) Cook until the sides appear set and bubbles form in the middle (about 2 to 3 minutes), then flip the pancake.
h) Once the pancake is cooked on that side, remove pancake from the heat and place on a plate.

88. Blueberry mango pancakes

Ingredients:
- 1 cup spelt flour
- ½ teaspoon baking powder
- ½ teaspoon baking soda
- ¾ cup plain Greek yogurt
- ¼ cup + 2 tablespoons 2% low-fat milk
- 1 large egg
- 2 tablespoons maple syrup
- ½ cup puréed mangoes
- ½ cup blueberries

Directions

a) Add the flour, baking powder, and baking soda to a bowl and whisk to combine.
b) In another bowl, whisk the yogurt, milk, egg, maple syrup, and puréed mango together until combined.
c) Add the wet Ingredients to the dry Ingredients and whisk until thoroughly combined.
d) Carefully stir in the blueberries.
e) Let the batter rest for 2 to 3 minutes. This allows all of the Ingredients to come together and gives the batter a better consistency.
f) Spray a non-stick skillet or griddle generously with vegetable oil and heat over medium heat.
g) Once the skillet is hot, add the batter using a ¼-cup measuring cup and pour the batter into the skillet to make the pancake. Use the measuring cup to help shape the pancake.
h) Cook until the sides appear set and bubbles form in the middle (about 2 to 3 minutes), then flip the pancake.
i) Once the pancake is cooked on that side, remove pancake from the heat and place on a plate.
j) Continue these steps with the rest of the batter.

89. Mocha pancakes

Ingredients:
- 1½ cups spelt flour
- ¼ cup unsweetened cocoa
- 3 teaspoons instant espresso powder
- 1½ teaspoons baking powder
- 1 teaspoon baking soda
- ½ teaspoon salt
- 2 tablespoons coconut oil, melted
- 1 teaspoon vanilla extract
- 2 large eggs, beaten
- 1¼ cups plain kefir

Directions

a) Add the spelt flour, cocoa, espresso powder, baking powder, baking soda, and salt to a bowl and whisk to combine.
b) In another bowl, whisk the coconut oil, vanilla, eggs, and kefir together until they are well combined. The melted coconut oil might harden up when combined with colder Ingredients, so you can slightly warm the kefir to help prevent this from happening if you'd like.
c) Add the wet Ingredients to the dry Ingredients and whisk until thoroughly combined.
d) Let the batter rest for 2 to 3 minutes. This allows all of the Ingredients to come together and gives the batter a better consistency.
e) Spray a non-stick skillet or griddle generously with vegetable oil and heat over medium heat.
f) Once the skillet is hot, add the batter using a ¼-cup measuring cup and pour the batter into the skillet to make the pancake. Use the measuring cup to help shape the pancake.
g) Cook until the sides appear set and bubbles form in the middle (about 2 to 3 minutes), then flip the pancake.
h) Once the pancake is cooked on that side, remove pancake from the heat and place on a plate.

90. Chai pancakes

Ingredients:
- 1½ cups quinoa flour
- 1½ teaspoons baking powder
- 1 teaspoon baking soda
- 1 teaspoon cinnamon
- ¾ teaspoon ground cardamom
- Generous pinch ground cloves
- ½ teaspoon ground ginger
- ½ teaspoon ground allspice
- ½ teaspoon salt
- 2 large eggs, beaten
- 2 tablespoons coconut oil, melted
- 1¼ cups plain kefir
- ¼ cup maple syrup
- 1 teaspoon vanilla extract

Directions

a) In a large bowl, add the flour, baking powder, baking soda, cinnamon, cardamom, cloves, ginger, allspice, and salt together and whisk to thoroughly combine.

b) In another bowl, whisk the eggs, coconut oil, kefir, maple syrup, and vanilla together until combined. The melted coconut oil might harden up when combined with colder Ingredients, so you can slightly warm the kefir to help prevent this from happening if you'd like.

c) Add the wet Ingredients to the dry Ingredients and whisk until thoroughly combined.

d) Let the batter rest for 2 to 3 minutes. This allows all of the Ingredients to come together and gives the batter a better consistency.

e) Spray a non-stick skillet or griddle generously with vegetable oil and heat over medium heat.

f) Once the skillet is hot, add the batter using a ¼-cup measuring cup and pour the batter into the skillet to make the pancake. Use the measuring cup to help shape the pancake.

g) Cook until the sides appear set and bubbles form in the middle (about 2 to 3 minutes), then flip the pancake.

h) Once the pancake is cooked on that side, remove pancake from the heat and place on a plate.

91. Carrot cake pancakes

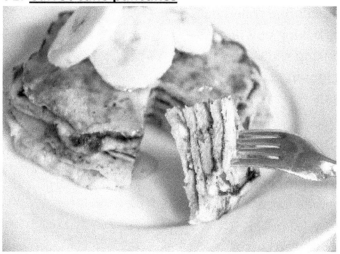

Ingredients:
- 1½ cups old-fashioned rolled oats
- 1½ teaspoons baking powder
- 1 teaspoon baking soda
- ½ teaspoon cinnamon
- ¼ teaspoon salt
- Dash of nutmeg
- 1 large egg
- 2 tablespoons coconut oil, melted
- 1 tablespoon maple syrup
- 1 teaspoon vanilla extract
- 1¼ cups 2% low-fat milk
- 1½ cups finely grated carrots
- ½ cup chopped golden raisins
- ½ cup chopped walnuts

Directions

a) Add all of the Ingredients, except for the carrots, raisins, and walnuts, to a blender. The melted coconut oil might harden up when combined with colder Ingredients, so you can slightly warm the milk to help prevent this from happening if you'd like.
b) Blitz everything in the blender until you have a smooth liquid.
c) Pour the pancake mixture into a large bowl.
d) Add the carrots, raisins, and walnuts to the batter and stir to thoroughly.
e) Let the batter rest for 5 to 10 minutes. This allows all of the Ingredients to come together and gives the batter a better consistency.
f) Spray a non-stick skillet or griddle generously with vegetable oil and heat over medium heat.
g) Once the skillet is hot, add the batter using a ¼-cup measuring cup and pour the batter into the skillet to make the pancake. Use the measuring cup to help shape the pancake.
h) Cook until the sides appear set and bubbles form in the middle, then flip the pancake.
i) Once the pancake is cooked on that side, remove pancake from the heat and place on a plate.

92. Honey banana pancakes

Ingredients:
- 1 ripe banana, plus more for serving
- 2 large eggs
- 1 tablespoon honey
- ½ teaspoon baking powder
- Maple syrup, for serving

Directions

a) Add the banana to a bowl and mash it until it's nice and creamy—no lumps.
b) Crack the eggs into another bowl and whisk until they are thoroughly mixed.
c) Add the honey and the baking powder to the bowl of banana and then pour in the eggs. Whisk to completely combine everything together.
d) Spray a non-stick skillet or griddle generously with vegetable oil and heat over medium heat.
e) Once the skillet is hot, add 2 tablespoons of batter into the skillet to make the pancake.
f) Cook until the sides appear set (you won't see any bubbles), then carefully flip the pancake.
g) Once the pancake is cooked on that side, remove the pancake from the heat and place on a plate.
h) Continue these steps with the rest of the batter.
i) Top with bananas and maple syrup.

93. Banana blueberry pancakes

Ingredients:
- 1 cup spelt flour
- ½ teaspoon baking powder
- ½ teaspoon baking soda
- 1 ripe medium banana, mashed
- ¾ cup plain Greek yogurt
- ¼ cup + 2 tablespoons 2% low-fat milk
- 1 large egg
- 2 tablespoons maple syrup
- ½ cup blueberries

Directions

a) Add the flour, baking powder, and baking soda to a bowl and whisk to combine.
b) In another bowl, whisk the mashed banana, yogurt, milk, egg, and maple syrup until combined.
c) Add the wet Ingredients to the dry Ingredients and whisk until thoroughly combined.
d) Carefully stir in the blueberries.
e) Let the batter rest for 2 to 3 minutes. This allows all of the Ingredients to come together and gives the batter a better consistency.
f) Spray a non-stick skillet or griddle generously with vegetable oil and heat over medium heat.
g) Once the skillet is hot, add the batter using a ¼-cup measuring cup and pour the batter into the skillet to make the pancake. Use the measuring cup to help shape the pancake.
h) Cook until the sides appear set and bubbles form in the middle (about 2 to 3 minutes), then flip the pancake.
i) Once the pancake is cooked on that side, remove pancake from the heat and place on a plate.
j) Continue these steps with the rest of the batter.

94. Apple cinnamon pancakes

Ingredients:
- 1¾ cups old-fashioned rolled oats
- 1½ teaspoons baking powder
- 1 teaspoon baking soda
- ¼ teaspoon cinnamon
- ¼ teaspoon salt
- 1 cup applesauce
- 2 tablespoons coconut oil, melted
- 1 tablespoon maple syrup
- 1 large egg
- 1 teaspoon vanilla extract
- ½ cup 2% low-fat milk

Directions

a) Add all of the Ingredients to blender. The melted coconut oil might harden up when combined with colder Ingredients, so you can slightly warm the milk to help prevent this from happening if you'd like.
b) Blitz everything in the blender until you have a smooth liquid.
c) Pour the pancake batter into a large bowl.
d) Let the batter rest for 5 to 10 minutes. This allows all of the Ingredients to come together and gives the batter a better consistency.
e) Spray a non-stick skillet or griddle generously with vegetable oil and heat over medium heat.
f) Once the skillet is hot, add the batter using a ¼-cup measuring cup and pour the batter into the skillet to make the pancake. Use the measuring cup to help shape the pancake.
g) Cook until the sides appear set and bubbles form in the middle (about 2 to 3 minutes), then flip the pancake.
h) Once the pancake is cooked on that side, remove pancake from the heat and place on a plate.
i) Continue these steps with the rest of the batter.

95. <u>Strawberry cheesecake pancakes</u>

Ingredients:
- 1 cup spelt flour
- 2 tablespoons sugar-free vanilla pudding mix
- ½ teaspoon baking powder
- ½ teaspoon baking soda
- ¾ cup plain Greek yogurt
- ½ cup + 2 tablespoons 2% low-fat milk
- 1 large egg
- 2 tablespoons maple syrup
- 1 cup thinly sliced strawberries

Directions

a) Add the flour, pudding mix, baking powder, and baking soda to a bowl and whisk to combine.
b) In another bowl, whisk the yogurt, milk, egg, and maple syrup until combined.
c) Add the wet Ingredients to the dry Ingredients and whisk until thoroughly combined.
d) Carefully stir in the strawberries.
e) Let the batter rest for 2 to 3 minutes. This allows all of the Ingredients to come together and gives the batter a better consistency.
f) Spray a non-stick skillet or griddle generously with vegetable oil and heat over medium heat.
g) Once the skillet is hot, add the batter using a ¼-cup measuring cup and pour the batter into the skillet to make the pancake. Use the measuring cup to help shape the pancake.
h) Cook until the sides appear set and bubbles form in the middle (about 2 to 3 minutes), then flip the pancake.
i) Once the pancake is cooked on that side, remove pancake from the heat and place on a plate.
j) Continue these steps with the rest of the batter.

96. Blueberry pancakes

Ingredients:
- 1¾ cups old-fashioned rolled oats
- 1½ teaspoons baking powder
- 1 teaspoon baking soda
- ½ teaspoon cinnamon
- ¼ teaspoon salt
- 1 large egg
- 2 tablespoons coconut oil, melted
- 1 tablespoon maple syrup
- 1 teaspoon vanilla extract
- 1¼ cups 2% low-fat milk
- ½ cup blueberries

Directions

a) Add all of the Ingredients, except for the blueberries, to the blender. The melted coconut oil might harden up when combined with colder Ingredients, so you can slightly warm the milk to help prevent this from happening if you'd like.
b) Blitz everything in the blender until you have a smooth liquid.
c) Pour the pancake mixture into a large bowl.
d) Carefully stir in the blueberries.
e) Let the batter rest for 5 to 10 minutes. This allows all of the Ingredients to come together and gives the batter a better consistency.
f) Spray a non-stick skillet or griddle generously with vegetable oil and heat over medium heat.
g) Once the skillet is hot, add the batter using a ¼-cup measuring cup and pour the batter into the skillet to make the pancake. Use the measuring cup to help shape the pancake.
h) Cook until the sides appear set and bubbles form in the middle (about 2 to 3 minutes), then flip the pancake.
i) Once the pancake is cooked on that side, remove pancake from the heat and place on a plate.
j) Continue these steps with the rest of the batter.

97. Strawberry banana pancakes

Ingredients:
- 1 cup spelt flour
- ½ teaspoon baking powder
- ½ teaspoon baking soda
- ¾ cup plain Greek yogurt
- 1 ripe medium banana, mashed
- ½ cup + 2 tablespoons 2% low-fat milk
- 1 large egg
- 2 tablespoons maple syrup
- ¾ cup sliced strawberries

Directions
a) Add the flour, baking powder, and baking soda to a bowl and whisk to combine.
b) In another bowl, whisk the yogurt, mashed banana, milk, egg, and maple syrup until combined.
c) Add the wet Ingredients to the dry Ingredients and whisk until thoroughly combined.
d) Carefully stir in the strawberries.
e) Let the batter rest for 2 to 3 minutes. This allows all of the Ingredients to come together and gives the batter a better consistency.
f) Spray a non-stick skillet or griddle generously with vegetable oil and heat over medium heat.
g) Once the skillet is hot, add the batter using a ¼-cup measuring cup and pour the batter into the skillet to make the pancake. Use the measuring cup to help shape the pancake.
h) Cook until the sides appear set and bubbles form in the middle (about 2 to 3 minutes), then flip the pancake.
i) Once the pancake is cooked on that side, remove pancake from the heat and place on a plate.
j) Continue these steps with the rest of the batter.

98. Peaches and cream pancakes

Ingredients:
- 1¾ cups old-fashioned rolled oats
- 2 tablespoons sugar-free vanilla pudding mix
- 1½ teaspoons baking powder
- 1 teaspoon baking soda
- ½ teaspoon cinnamon
- ¼ teaspoon salt
- 1 tablespoon butter, melted
- 1 large egg
- ¼ cup 2% low-fat milk
- 1 teaspoon vanilla extract
- 2 cups peeled and sliced peaches (if using frozen peaches, thaw them first)

Directions

a) Add all of the Ingredients to a blender.
b) Blitz everything in the blender until you have a smooth liquid.
c) Pour the pancake batter into a large bowl.
d) Let the batter rest for 5 to 10 minutes. This allows all of the Ingredients to come together and gives the batter a better consistency.
e) Spray a non-stick skillet or griddle generously with vegetable oil and heat over medium-low heat.
f) Once the skillet is hot, add the batter using a ¼-cup measuring cup and pour the batter into the skillet to make the pancake. Use the measuring cup to help shape the pancake.
g) Cook until the sides appear set and bubbles form in the middle (about 2 to 3 minutes), then flip the pancake.
h) Once the pancake is cooked on that side, remove pancake from the heat and place on a plate.
i) Continue these steps with the rest of the batter.

99. Banana bread pancakes

Ingredients:
- 1 cup spelt flour
- ½ teaspoon baking powder
- ½ teaspoon baking soda
- ¾ cup plain Greek yogurt
- 1 ripe medium banana, mashed
- ½ cup + 2 tablespoons 2% low-fat milk
- 1 large egg
- 2 tablespoons maple syrup

Directions
a) Add the flour, baking powder, and baking soda to a bowl and whisk to combine.
b) In another bowl, whisk the yogurt, mashed banana, milk, egg, and maple syrup until combined.
c) Add the wet Ingredients to the dry Ingredients and whisk until combined.
d) Let the batter rest for 2 to 3 minutes. This allows all of the Ingredients to come together and gives the batter a better consistency.
e) Spray a non-stick skillet or griddle generously with vegetable oil and heat over medium heat.
f) Once the skillet is hot, add the batter using a ¼-cup measuring cup and pour the batter into the skillet to make the pancake. Use the measuring cup to help shape the pancake.
g) Cook until the sides appear set and bubbles form in the middle (about 2 to 3 minutes), then flip the pancake.
h) Once the pancake is cooked on that side, remove pancake from the heat and place on a plate.
i) Continue these steps with the rest of the batter.

100. Tropical pancakes

Ingredients:
- 1¾ cups old-fashioned rolled oats
- 1½ teaspoons baking powder
- 1 teaspoon baking soda
- ½ teaspoon cinnamon
- ¼ teaspoon salt
- 1 ripe medium banana, mashed
- 2 tablespoons coconut oil, melted
- 1 tablespoon maple syrup
- 1 large egg
- 1 teaspoon vanilla extract
- ¾ cup 2% low-fat milk
- ½ cup canned full-fat coconut milk
- ½ cup finely diced pineapple (if using frozen, make sure it's been thawed)
- ½ cup finely diced mango (if using frozen, make sure it's been thawed)

Directions

a) Add all of the Ingredients, except the pineapple and mango, to a blender. The melted coconut oil might harden up when combined with colder Ingredients, so you can slightly warm the milk to help prevent this from happening if you'd like.
b) Blitz the mixture in the blender until you have a smooth liquid.
c) Pour the pancake batter into a large bowl.
d) Stir in the pineapple and mango.
e) Let the batter rest for 5 to 10 minutes. This allows all of the Ingredients to come together and gives the batter a better consistency.
f) Spray a non-stick skillet or griddle generously with vegetable oil and heat over medium-low heat.
g) Once the skillet is hot, add the batter using a ¼-cup measuring cup and pour the batter into the skillet to make the pancake. Use the measuring cup to help shape the pancake.
h) Cook until the sides appear set and bubbles form in the middle (about 2 to 3 minutes), then flip the pancake.
i) Once the pancake is cooked on that side, remove pancake from the heat and place on a plate.

CONCLUSION

Crepes and pancakes are not only delicious, but also a great way to start your day. With so many variations and ingredients to choose from, they can be customized to suit any taste or dietary preference. So why not try out a new recipe and enjoy a delicious and satisfying breakfast or brunch?

Milton Keynes UK
Ingram Content Group UK Ltd.
UKHW020703050923
428087UK00017B/1266